overcome problem eating

A PRACTICAL GUIDE TO TREATING EATING DISORDERS

PATRICIA FURNESS-SMITH

This edition published in the UK
in 2019 by Icon Books Ltd,
Omnibus Business Centre,
39–41 North Road,
London N7 9DP
email: info@iconbooks.com
www.iconbooks.com

First published in the UK
in 2014 by Icon Books

Sold in the UK, Europe and Asia
by Faber & Faber Ltd,
Bloomsbury House,
74–77 Great Russell Street,
London WC1B 3DA
or their agents

Distributed in South Africa
by Jonathan Ball,
Office B4, The District,
41 Sir Lowry Road,
Woodstock 7925

Distributed in Australia and
New Zealand
by Allen & Unwin Pty Ltd,
PO Box 8500,
83 Alexander Street,
Crows Nest,
NSW 2065

Distributed in Canada
by Publishers Group Canada,
76 Stafford Street, Unit 300
Toronto,
Ontario M6J 2S1

Distributed in the USA
by Publishers Group West,
1700 Fourth Street,
Berkeley, CA 94710

ISBN: 978-178578-466-8

Typeset in Avenir by Marie Doherty

Printed and bound in Great Britain by Clays Ltd, Elcograf S.p.A.

About the author

Patricia Furness-Smith is a psychologist and accredited practitioner with over 25 years of experience in clinical practice. She has lectured and trained in psychology, psychotherapy and psychopathology in higher and further education institutions and has held a variety of roles: clinical supervisor; moderator; examiner; reviewer and validator. She is a magistrate and a Fellow of the National Counselling Society (NCS).

As well as running her own private practice, she is a freelance writer and consultant on British Airways' 'Flying with Confidence' courses. She is the co-author of *Flying with Confidence: The Proven Programme to Fix your Flying Fears* and sole author of the guided relaxation CD of the same title. Her particular specialisms are in relationships, eating disorders and phobias. She is also the author of *A Practical Guide to Well-being* and *A Practical Guide to Overcoming Phobias*.

She enjoys an international reputation as a specialist in hodophobia (the fear of travelling). She is often quoted in the media and has appeared in national and foreign newspapers and magazines and on radio, television and social media sites.

Author's note

In order to respect client privacy and anonymity within the case studies described, I have formed composite characters by scrambling personal details and changing names.

Dedication

This book is dedicated to all the brave clients I have met over the years who have taken the necessary courageous steps to take back control of their lives by addressing their problem eating.

I would also like to extend my dedication to the wonderful team of volunteers, past and present, who generously offer their time and resources to the charity Eating Disorders Support. Their contributions – be it as helpline volunteers, self-help group facilitators, committee members, secretary, marketing and finance support, fundraisers, educators, policymakers or general dogsbodies – are all deeply valued and hugely appreciated.

Finally, this dedication would not be complete without particular mention of a very special, spritely octogenarian, Angela Loewi. It has been Angela's vision and determination to reach out to those who suffer from problem eating that has formed the backbone of the charity over the past decade and beyond. Angela deserves recognition for the inordinate amount of time and effort she has personally contributed, borne of her unswayable belief that someone must be there when people desperately need help. I can personally vouch for the fact that this indomitable, redoubtable and singularly stubborn lady has saved many lives, and we have the grateful letters and emails from survivors that prove it. She is an inspiration to us all with her tireless energy, enthusiasm and inability to accept defeat despite the paucity of services available for this cause. I wholeheartedly salute all the good she has achieved. I know that she will continue to lobby for better resources and education into problem eating right up to her very last breath.

> *I am only one, but I am one. I cannot do everything, but I can do something. And because I cannot do everything, I will not refuse to do the something that I can do.*
> Edward Everett Hale

Contents

Preface

*Nothing would be more tiresome than
eating and drinking if God had not made
them a pleasure as well as a necessity.*
Voltaire

Although the overwhelming majority of us would agree with Voltaire, there exists a sizeable percentage of the population for whom eating is not a pleasure but a source of considerable distress.

According to the National Institute of Health and Clinical Excellence (NICE), a conservative estimate of the number of people in the United Kingdom who suffer from an eating disorder is well in excess of 1.5 million. But it is recognized that these statistics do not take into account those with eating disorders who have not sought medical attention, are being treated in the community or are receiving private treatment. In addition, these statistics do not include those who suffer from what is known as 'disordered eating' – conditions similar to eating disorders but towards the milder end of the spectrum. We live in a conflicted world where obesity is on the rise as well as eating disorders, and the real extent of problems with eating is far greater than the figures convey.

Whether the issue is a full-blown eating disorder or problem eating, in many countries there is often both a profound lack of resources and, even more worryingly, a severe lack of understanding of the need for early diagnosis and treatment. Treatment for problem eating is practically non-existent, and sufferers of eating disorders must meet stringent criteria before they are entitled to treatment. By this stage, when their illness is sufficiently severe, a considerable amount of damage has already been caused that could easily have been avoided by earlier intervention.

Prevention and early detection are always far cheaper options in terms of both personal and financial cost.

Who is at risk of eating problems?

The National Eating Disorders Collaboration of Australia cites 9 per cent of the population as suffering from an eating disorder, and around the world problem eating is affecting increasingly younger populations. According to the Canadian Mental Health Association, 40 per cent of nine-year-old girls have tried to lose weight. Similarly alarming statistics are seen worldwide, and there is no doubt that body image issues and problem eating have increased over recent decades.

The escalation in problem eating is worrying enough for the individuals concerned, but we must also factor into the equation the inordinate distress this causes for the families and friends of the sufferer, especially in those cases where the sufferer has not yet sought, or been allocated, appropriate help.

And that's why I've written this book. Clearly, it would be impossible to cover specific eating problems in tremendous depth or give detailed explanations of the various treatments available in such a small book as this. However, it is my fervent belief as a practitioner that there is an urgent need for a simple, down-to-earth book to address this dangerous and escalating problem. My intention is to provide accessible information about the different types of problem eating, which will promote a general understanding of problem eating along with an awareness of the treatments available and where to find help. Whether you are worried about your own eating or the eating of a relative, partner or friend, I hope you'll find reassurance and assistance here.

 Despite these alarming and escalating trends in the incidence of problematic eating, there is also every reason to be positive, since eating distress can be overcome, providing that it is recognized and treated.

In the past, educational messages have enabled us to make informed choices about whether we choose to indulge in smoking, binge drinking or recreational drug-taking, having had the consequences spelled out to us. But similar knowledge about problem eating is thin on the ground, and it's my hope that by having the requisite knowledge about triggers which may lead to problem eating, we are more likely to shun these destructive behaviours in the first place.

There are a number of books available on the subject of eating disorders, many of them written by research academics, medical experts and numerous specialists in the field, offering insight into problem eating from their various philosophical orientations and approaches. Other books are written from the personal standpoint of individual sufferers or carers, who generously share their unique journeys through the landscape of problematic eating. Many of these books have great value in describing specific eating difficulties and will inform the reader of the minutiae of how to recognize and treat the specific eating disorder under discussion.

But this book is different because it provides a simple overview to enable you to recognize the wide variety of types of problem eating. It also includes information regarding the latest diagnostic criteria used to define an eating disorder, early warning signs and available treatments for specific eating disorders.

This book is intended to be an easily accessible resource for all those who are suffering from problem eating, caring for someone with eating distress or providing support in an educational or medical capacity to others on this subject.

In addition, parents, teachers, youth workers, school matrons, doctors, nurses, counsellors and psychotherapists are the intended audience for this book. Finally, this book is also aimed at interested members of the general public, who wish to augment their understanding of problem eating.

I have arranged this book in two parts. In part one, I will be exploring our relationship with food and the potential triggers, causes and history of different types of problem eating. I will then discuss four of the most common types of eating disorder: anorexia nervosa, bulimia nervosa, binge eating disorder and pica disorder. If you know you are dealing with one of these in particular, you might want to just read that section, but otherwise I would recommend reading them all to find out which parts apply to you. In the second part of the book, I will cover the various treatments available, along with other methods of help. And finally, we will look at how carers can support sufferers with problematic eating. At the very back of the book is a list of useful contacts and advice on where to go next.

As in all things in life, forewarned is forearmed. By knowing the signs and symptoms of problem eating, early detection is facilitated, thus enabling people to seek help sooner rather than later. Indeed, by knowing the serious consequences of these debilitating illnesses, I hope that many people will be empowered to avoid them in the first place.

 To solve a problem you must first acknowledge it, understand it and acquire the knowledge and skills needed to defeat it.

Only the educated are free.
Epictetus

6

PART ONE
Understanding Problem Eating

1. What is problem eating?

When you first looked at the title of this book, perhaps you were puzzled. What does 'problem eating' actually mean? You might have asked yourself, 'do I have a problem?', or perhaps you're curious to find out whether someone you know, whose eating behaviour is odd, has a real problem.

Opinions range far and wide as to whether problem eating relates to what we eat, how much we eat, how often we eat, or the time that we eat, and so on and so forth. In truth, all of these factors may play a part; problem eating is a spectrum ranging from the temporary, developmentally acceptable faddishness of a seven-year-old who only wants to eat hot dogs, right through to recognized mental health disorders such as bulimia nervosa. (Please note that for the purposes of this book the terms 'anorexia' and 'bulimia' should be taken to mean 'anorexia nervosa' and 'bulimia nervosa'.)

What is disordered eating?
In this book I will talk about both 'disordered eating' and 'eating disorders'. On the problem eating scale, eating disorders are at the severe end and disordered eating is at the milder end, though it can still be very damaging. Disordered

eating is far more prevalent than eating disorders are and consists of an enormously varied range of irregular eating patterns.

Some of these behaviours are relatively benign and short-lived, and while they can lead to weight gain or weight loss, they do not necessitate professional interventions as they are not psychologically damaging.

This category could include people who are building up their muscle tone in anticipation of running a marathon, actors losing weight to look the part for a particular role, people shedding a few pounds in anticipation of a beach holiday or brides-to-be trying to lose weight before their weddings. Future brides prove to be particularly susceptible to this, and a relative of mine even refers to it as 'getting down to marrying weight'! In a similar vein, I have had a number of clients who have been refused operations until they have lost sufficient weight to make the intended surgery less risky and more viable. Or someone might be neglectful about eating regular meals because they are obsessively busy with a project, ecstatically in love or feeling under the weather. The reasons why we eat irregularly are legion and are *usually* done on a consciously temporary basis.

When disordered eating becomes a problem

Disordered eating becomes harmful when our unusual habits regarding food begin to have a psychological effect on us. The most common issue here is the use of food to comfort, celebrate, reward or punish. Many people might overeat or under-eat from time to time in response to stress or sadness. They use food as a means of comforting or punishing themselves, or they may eat excessively as a way of celebrating or rewarding themselves. I often refer to this as the 'mood-food trigger', as palatable foods with an addictive quality release endorphins, dopamine and other chemicals that result in feelings of well-being, thus temporarily alleviating stress and pain.

Eating can be used as a replacement activity when we are trying to avoid facing up to our problems. Instead of using food to nourish our body we use it to silence our pain, frustration and anger.

Some of these triggers are more common than others. For example, in January there is usually a backlash against the over-indulgence of December, which results in shoals of people enrolling in gyms and abstaining from alcohol consumption in an attempt to lose the extra pounds gained. And even the most scrupulously regimented person may occasionally skip breakfast if they have slept in. All of these examples demonstrate a degree of disordered eating.

Although you may not have an eating disorder, many of us still feel out of control around food and experience discontent about our bodies or shame about our hunger. These are the prime causes of disordered eating.

Disordered eating
Stress and neglect

Marcia's 75-year-old husband, Oswald, suffered a severe heart attack while they were on holiday in Europe. Fortunately, he was taken to hospital in time and underwent life-saving surgery. Once released from hospital, Oswald was transferred to a rehabilitation centre where he remained for several months. During this time, Marcia visited Oswald daily and returned to her hotel accommodation each evening too distraught and exhausted to look after her own needs.

Marcia skipped breakfast and would arrive at the rehabilitation centre first thing in the morning to keep her husband company throughout the entire day. Apart from a cup of coffee and a sandwich at lunchtime, Marcia neglected to eat and retired straight to bed on her return to the hotel each evening.

As soon as Oswald was deemed fit enough to travel, the couple returned to their home in England. They both underwent health checks by their family doctor, which showed that Oswald's condition was stable and Marcia was slightly anaemic. Marcia had lost over a stone in weight as a result of the stress she had been under. The GP recommended that Marcia should take iron tablets and eat a healthy balanced diet, and within a few months Marcia regained the stone in weight.

In this instance, Marcia's disordered eating had nothing to do with her body image or a desire to lose weight. Her failure to eat appropriately was purely down to self-neglect as a consequence of her preoccupation about her husband's serious health scare.

What is an eating disorder?

An eating disorder is a far more serious condition than disordered eating, and thankfully it is far less common. An eating disorder, described at the simplest level, involves an unhealthy and obsessive preoccupation with food, which can manifest itself in excessive concerns about calorie intake, weight, exercise, purging, bingeing and body image.

The key factor of eating disorders is that they can radically interfere in a harmful way with how an individual engages with their social life, family life and working life, as well as how they perceive themself. An eating disorder negatively impacts on all four of the key domains: how we are physically, mentally, emotionally and behaviourally.

An obvious example of this would be a person suffering from the eating disorder anorexia. The brain alone requires approximately 500 calories per day to function effectively. Sufferers of anorexia frequently consume significantly fewer calories than this. As a consequence of the lack of nutrients, physical changes take place in the brain structure which cause a negative knock-on effect to the individual's social functioning – for instance, decreasing their ability to concentrate, learn and remember, among other issues.

Although eating disorders can happen to anyone, there are some groups of people who are more at risk than others. Risk factors for developing an eating disorder include:

- Being female

- Being an adolescent

- Being a perfectionist

- Being competitive

- Having low self-esteem

- Fearing conflict

- Being worried about others' opinions

- Being a people-pleaser

- Having anxiety or depression

- Having poor coping strategies

- Being unable to express emotions

- Being fearful about adult responsibility

- Being subjected to intense pressure to succeed

- Belonging to a profession that sets great store on body image and weight, for example models, athletes, dancers, skaters, synchronized swimmers and jockeys

- Having family members or peers with an eating disorder

- Coming from a family where overt dieting is promoted

- Having parents who are substance abusers, mentally ill, alcoholics, overly controlling or emotionally detached

- Being or having been obese

- Having been abused, neglected or bullied

- Having suffered trauma

- Being confused about sexual identity.

Why is problem eating more common in women?

In the relatively recent past, problem eating was seen as a predominantly female issue, with the ratio of male-to-female sufferers being roughly 1:10. But the 2007 Adult Psychiatric Morbidity Study revealed a dramatic change in this demographic, with 25 per cent of those suffering from eating distress being male. Still, the majority of sufferers are female, and there are a number of proposed reasons for this, including:

- The greater emphasis placed on females with regard to the importance of how they look

- Greater right brain activity in females than in males, which enables them to be more intuitive but also more susceptible to social comparison. This is particularly damaging in cultures that promote an ideal size for women, e.g. size 10. There is no such equivalent ideal size for men.

- The encouragement of the role of nurturer in females makes them more tuned in to meeting other people's needs and guilty about meeting their own. This makes them more vulnerable to food abuse as a coping mechanism for meeting their own unmet wants.

- In some cultures, females are seen as less important than males and may not have the same degree of autonomy. Their desire for control over their life may be displaced by control over their food intake.

Anorexia
Sub-type: Binge eating and purging type
Yanis was the youngest of four boys whose parents were both sports professionals. They had been successful competitors in their youths and now earned their living by offering coaching in their respective fields of expertise. Yanis's two eldest brothers, Antoine and Julien, followed in their parents' footsteps and acquitted themselves with honour on the sports field, as well as winning individual events in tennis and gymnastics.

But Guillaume, the third brother and six years older than Yanis, suffered from asthma attacks, which demanded a great deal of attention from Yanis's busy parents. As a consequence, Yanis frequently found that his parents were unable to take him to his gym classes. Yanis loved these classes and showed as much, if not more, promise than his two oldest brothers. But as Guillaume's health deteriorated, Yanis missed more and more classes and eventually was taken off the junior squad due to not achieving the minimum attendance rate in accordance with the club rules.

Yanis was devastated by this and began to assuage his frustration by comfort eating. Although at one level he understood the reasons why his parents could not ferry him to classes, he nevertheless felt insignificant and neglected. It seemed that all his brothers had received more of his parents' attention and that he was just less important than the others.

Approximately six months after leaving the squad, Yanis and his family attended the championship in which his brother Antoine was competing. At the event he bumped into some of his old squad mates who were unable to conceal their surprise at the considerable amount of weight Yanis had put on since they had last met. He saw the junior squad captain, Jerome, point in his direction and then loudly whisper to his friend, Evan, 'The Incredible Hulk!' He recoiled at their subsequent laughter and felt ashamed and humiliated at how he was now perceived by his former squad-mates.

From that day, Yanis made a pledge to himself that he would lose weight, so that he would never again be the butt of unkind jokes about his appearance. Immediately,

Yanis started to restrict his food intake to a level significantly below the requirements for a developing teenage boy. This, not unnaturally, caused him to experience acute pangs of hunger, which reached a level of such discomfort that he would then capitulate and eat excessively. Immediately after bingeing, the guilt and shame he experienced at the prospect of becoming fat became totally unbearable. So intense and obsessive was his fear of gaining weight that he fell into the habit of purging by self-induced vomiting and excessive exercising.

Yanis's schoolwork began to deteriorate and he steadily withdrew from all of his friendship groups. Increasingly Yanis's free time was taken up with long solitary runs in the evening or being alone in his bedroom, claiming that he was tired or had a headache. The family had noticed Yanis's mood swings and lack of sociability but had put it down to the fact that he was going through adolescence.

Thankfully, Guillaume eventually became suspicious about Yanis's instant visits to the bathroom after having eaten and challenged his younger brother. By this stage, Yanis's weight had fallen considerably below the recommended BMI for his age and height. Yanis confided in Guillaume about his hurt and disappointment at having to give up gymnastics and his humiliation by Jerome.

Guillaume, as a result of his own experience with illness, listened to Yanis with patience and empathy and managed to persuade him to tell his parents immediately. They were aghast when they heard about their youngest child's suffering and took instant steps to get the necessary help for Yanis.

As Yanis was given cognitive behavioural therapy (which will be discussed in chapter 11) to overcome anorexia at such an early stage, he made a relatively rapid recovery. This was also due in part to his parents' promise that he could resume gymnastic training as soon as he was fit and well enough to do so.

As we shall see later in the book, one of the prime motivations for helping someone recover from any eating disorder is to put the sufferer back in touch with themself as a whole, unique person, not just a physical entity, obsessed with weight and body shape. Yanis was lucky that he had something in his life that he felt passionately about, and this was his love of gymnastics. By recognizing his own abilities and talents, Yanis had the determination and strength to quell the anorexic voice in his head and re-establish his own autonomy. Yanis was also fortunate in having the support of his siblings and parents, who played a key role in helping him towards recovery.

An eating disorder is a type of mental illness

An eating disorder is largely used to displace painful emotions, which the sufferer feels unable to face, thus affording them a temporary sense of control, relief or release. This sense of control, albeit false and a form of self-harm, becomes all-consuming and is in short a mental illness.

THINK ABOUT IT

People do not develop an eating disorder by conscious choice but rather as an unconscious protection from emotional pain.

Examples of such eating disorders are binge eating disorder, anorexia and bulimia. Notable exceptions to the description of an eating disorder in the previous section are conditions such as **rumination disorder** or **avoidant/restrictive food intake disorder**, in which concern for body image and shape is not a factor.

REMEMBER THIS!!!

An eating disorder is analogous to tears or laughter in that it is merely a symptom or sign of the individual's emotional state. To offer a handkerchief to wipe away tears, without finding out why the person is upset, is as superficial as trying to treat an eating disorder by regulating the food intake without addressing the underlying emotional issues.

Can dieting lead to an eating disorder?

It is important to note that sometimes people fall into an eating disorder as a result of disordered eating practices, such as embarking on a particularly stringent diet. However, it must be stressed that not all people who diet go on to develop eating disorders.

Dieting in some countries (including the UK) has become a commonplace cultural behaviour, accompanied by a strong sense of social endorsement that confers status upon people who try to achieve slimness. Because of social pressure to conform to a particular ideal of how one should look, a number of people, due to their personality and other factors, may internalize this ideal and become obsessed with it. These are the people who may be at risk of turning their diet, or their mildly disordered eating, into a full-blown eating disorder.

THINK ABOUT IT

Why do many people believe that being thin is more important than being healthy?

Despite trying diet after diet and failing to maintain their ideal weight, the dieter persists and tries yet another diet. It seems extraordinary that the individual blames themself, rather than blaming dieting. The hallmark of sanity is recognizing that if what you are doing does not give you the results that you want then it is time to try something different. One of the biggest problems with failed dieting is that it creates a rebound effect, which leads to appetite increase. This can lead to increased weight gain, and so the whole cycle starts again.

One important factor in the development of eating disorders is the addictive potential of food. Janet Treasure, Professor of Psychiatry at Guy's, Kings and St Thomas' School of Medicine in London and leading expert on eating disorders, has warned of the changes in the brain caused by alternating between feasting and fasting.

This form of eating pattern leads to changes in the opiate and dopamine receptors, which in layman's terms means we can develop an 'addicted brain'. Knowing this fact would make many of us think twice before yo-yoing between starving ourselves then over-indulging by eating to excess, which is often the pattern that occurs with dieting.

Addictions of any type are difficult to overcome, as those who have tried to give up nicotine or alcohol can attest. It is astounding how many men, women and children unwittingly stumble into addiction, and what may appear to be an innocuous diet can trigger serious consequences in some people.

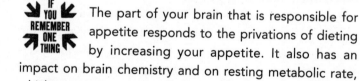 The part of your brain that is responsible for appetite responds to the privations of dieting by increasing your appetite. It also has an impact on brain chemistry and on resting metabolic rate, which promotes overeating. These are survival mechanisms, with which you cannot argue.

In addition, yo-yo dieting actually causes people to put on weight, since the body will automatically hoard calories.

This is not dissimilar to those of us who have experienced being temporarily financially strapped for cash. As a result of this inconvenience, during affluent times we tend to put a little aside for a rainy day; your body does exactly the same thing. But instead of it being a wad of notes under the mattress, it is a wad of fat around the waist!

2. Overcoming ignorance and offering hope

Real knowledge is to know the
extent of one's ignorance.
Confucius

Help for sufferers and carers

I have worked with clients who have suffered with problematic eating for over twenty years, and in the past fourteen years I have been intimately involved with this issue in my current role as a clinical supervisor and trainer for a charity known as Eating Disorders Support.

This charity provides a daily telephone and email helpline, along with the facilitation of fortnightly self-help groups for sufferers, carers or those from any walk of life who wish to learn more about the experiences of those who live with problematic eating. Working with this charity has made me painfully aware of the lack of help available for many sufferers of problem eating. We are frequently contacted by people from all over the world who sadly are unable to get the support they need from their own continent. In reality there is often a serious dearth of support for sufferers of eating distress.

But as well as treating sufferers of problem eating, I frequently work with the parents, partners, colleagues, friends and adult children of sufferers. They, like the sufferer, need support, since the emotional demands placed upon them can be very intense. They often feel that they can't do right for doing wrong when trying to offer help to the sufferer. Many family members describe the household dynamics when living with someone with problem eating as being like permanently walking on eggshells.

Friends and family can be terrified that they might make matters worse by commenting on changed behaviours, such as excessive exercising or the refusal to eat various food groups. The mere mention of weight loss or gain can lead to tears and tantrums. Mealtimes can become a dreaded battleground causing distress and anxiety for the entire family.

Being in a family with someone suffering from problem eating, particularly if you are the primary carer, can be a lonely journey, fraught with frustration, despair and isolation. Sometimes you might feel that there is a glimmer of light at the end of the tunnel, only to have your hopes cruelly dashed by a relapse.

In many cases, problem eating can become the focal point of the entire family's existence, causing their regular social life to dwindle as it becomes difficult to invite people to the home. Holidays may be put on hold, food and menus dominate, arguments become a regular occurrence and family members feel permanently tense and bullied.

Problem eating doesn't just affect the sufferer. Relatives, partners and friends all suffer too, but they can also offer valuable support when it comes to recovery.

A need for increased awareness
It still shocks me to discover that many members of the public who have not been personally touched by an eating disorder perceive these mental health illnesses in a pejorative and highly inaccurate fashion.

I have frequently heard eating disorders being described as: voluntary lifestyle choices, evidence of a greedy disposition, manifestations of vanity, proof of lack of self-control and attention-seeking. All of these beliefs woefully miss the mark and undermine the seriousness of these dangerous conditions.

 People suffering from an eating disorder have a serious mental illness and are deserving of the same level of respect, support and attention as someone seeking help for a physical condition. If you think you might have a problem, you deserve and need help in the same way you would if you were injured or physically ill.

A need for a culture change
The ignorance and misunderstanding surrounding eating problems is further compounded by the fact, in my sad and

frustrating experience, that a considerable proportion of the medical profession does not possess a solid grasp of the aetiology, process or treatment of problematic eating. Problematic eating has long been the poor relation within the mental health field, perceived by many as self-inflicted.

I have heard accounts of sufferers of eating disorders who, having taken the courageous step to reach out for medical support, have been told by their GPs to, 'just go away and eat' or that 'your BMI [which we will look at in chapter 9] is not low enough to warrant help'.

Obviously there are many good doctors out there, and I don't want to put you off seeking medical help, but it is shocking that this dismissive attitude persists, especially since there is compelling scientific evidence that genetics plays a significant role in eating disorders. For example, there is a 55 per cent concordance of anorexia in identical twins compared to a 5 per cent concordance in fraternal twins.

 Brian Lask, President of the Eating Disorders Research Society, has discovered a very interesting phenomenon, which sheds light on the theory that some people have a genetic predisposition to develop an eating disorder.

When someone starves themself, all major organs in the body shrink, including the brain. By using neuro-imagery, Lask discovered that once a healthy body weight has been restored, everything goes back to normal except one crucial area of the brain: the insula. The insula plays a key role in how we perceive taste, control anxiety, maintain an accurate body image, receive hunger and satiety cues and sense pain.

A dysfunctional insula explains why a severely emaciated person can feel that they are hugely fat when clearly they are not. It also explains how a malnourished person can push themself to exercise, despite physical injuries, since their pain tolerance threshold has shot through the roof.

This neurological research casts light on why some people who diet develop an eating disorder while others do not. Whether it is because someone is born with a faulty insula, or whether extreme starvation causes permanent damage to this essential part of the brain, remains to be decided. Whichever of the two hypotheses is correct, it clearly demonstrates the perniciousness of starvation diets.

To my absolute horror, I recently heard the following statement on a morning TV programme from a GP who was responding to a caller who had enquired if an eating disorder would remain on her medical record. He replied:

> *Yes, it will be in your medical records; it's on your medical history forever. It will be there as a black mark, as a stigma … it shouldn't be but it is.*

This thoughtless comment would, I'm sure, have undermined the likelihood of this caller seeking help and would have deterred many sufferers from coming forward for help rather than risk being stigmatized.

Be determined and persistent when seeking help

In fairness to GPs, one should not expect them to be specialists in every field. However, even though it is accepted practice, I think it's awful that in the case of eating disorders patients are told that they need to become sicker before they will be entitled to treatment. If you were worried you were an alcoholic, you wouldn't expect your doctor to tell you to come back when your liver was sufficiently damaged.

That's why early diagnosis of problem eating is key – the longer the unhealthy eating habits prevail, the harder it is to dislodge them, and the more damage is done.

 The mortality rate from eating disorders is the highest of all mental illnesses. This is partly due to physical reasons such as heart failure, malnutrition or other organ failure. However, a huge proportion of deaths are due to suicide. Early intervention is absolutely crucial.

It is my belief that the younger generation of doctors and other medical professionals is much more aware of how eating disorders can ravage lives. This is due to many of them having experienced the damage caused by these disorders first-hand, within their own friendship circles or among fellow classmates at school, college and university.

However, there are still a number of dinosaurs out there. If you do not get the response you need, do not give up. I suggest that you make another appointment immediately, but this time take someone with you for moral support or to act as an advocate in expressing your right to have timely and effective help.

 If you're worried about your eating habits, have you ever spoken to your doctor about it? If not, book an appointment now. You might be pleasantly surprised by the outcome.

Message of hope

I know this all sounds a bit doom-and-gloom, but one of the most important things I want you to take away from this book is that problematic eating – from inconsequential pregnancy cravings to acknowledged serious mental health disorders such as binge eating disorder or anorexia – can be overcome.

The earlier the intervention takes place to halt the problem eating, the better the prognosis. However, people with long-standing and deeply entrenched eating disorders can still make a full recovery, providing they are given the appropriate treatment.

Sufferers can move on to lead full, healthy, joyous lives, freed from the enslaving shackles of the eating disorder's

28

tyranny. For many, the reign of an eating disorder can be terminated permanently, although some practitioners would have you believe otherwise.

I have often heard people claim that there is no total cure to an eating disorder and sufferers remain susceptible for the rest of their life. It is a similar philosophy to the expression 'once an alcoholic, always an alcoholic'. However, Janet Treasure, a professor of psychiatry at Guys, King's & St Thomas Medical School in London, recently stated that eating disorders 'can be completely cured, especially if they are treated during the first three years'.

Each sufferer is unique, and while one treatment might work well for one person, it may prove to be unsuitable for another. In fact, I am aware of many cases where people have needed a range of professional treatments before achieving recovery. In other cases people have overcome their problem eating without professional help and have achieved recovery through self-help books, coupled with the support of family and friends.

Problem eating in the 21st century

Today, there is no doubt that the number of people experiencing problem eating has escalated enormously, which is both alarming and disheartening. However, on the positive side, the number of sufferers who are now openly admitting to having experienced an eating disorder is on the increase too.

Suffering from problem eating can be extremely iso-
lating, since many people feel embarrassed about sharing
their habits and behaviours with others. To know that you
are not alone is very empowering, particularly for younger
people who worry more about being different from their
peers.

A gradual cultural change is happening and rather than
denying that mental health issues such as eating disorders
exist, people are coming forward and sharing their experiences. This openness helps to educate the general public
to be vigilant in recognizing the symptoms, and encourages
them to take action at the earliest stage to get help.

Don't wait until tomorrow; take action *now*

If you are suffering from eating distress, I strongly urge you
to take the necessary steps to address the problem now, in
order for you to start living your life with you at the helm.
This might mean confiding in a friend, picking up the phone
to call a helpline or making an appointment to see your GP.

Taking these first steps to seek help takes courage, but
the rewards in doing so are quite spectacular. Having con-
quered an eating disorder, survivors are confident in the
knowledge that they possess the resources to overcome
whatever challenges life may throw at them.

*Adversity has the effect of eliciting talents which in
prosperous circumstances would have lain dormant.*
Horace

3. Our relationship with food

*One cannot think well, love well, sleep
well, if one has not dined well.*
Virginia Woolf

In this chapter we will look at the many factors that influence our relationship with food and how these change over time. Variables such as choice, availability, individual requirements, nutritional advice, affordability, marketing and advertising are just some of the plethora of influences on how we eat.

One of the complicating factors with problem eating is that, unlike dealing with problems such as addictions to alcohol, pornography or gambling, or drug or substance abuse, we cannot simply *abstain* from the offending behaviour.

In the same way that we need air to breathe, shelter to provide us with protection from the elements and water to prevent us from dehydration, we all need food to provide the essential fuel for growth, movement and development.

In disordered eating and eating disorders, food is both the problem and the solution.

There are many different ways to abuse our need to eat

We can abuse this basic requirement for food by over- or under-consumption, along with further abuse by consuming an excess of a particular type of food and too little of other necessary food types, leading to harmful vitamin or mineral deficiencies within our bodies.

Sometimes we abuse our need to eat by eating irregularly, yo-yoing from long stints of starvation to bursts of uncontrolled bingeing. In other cases the abuse takes the form of ingestion of harmful non-nutritive substances, which can cause serious physical complications. This latter eating disorder is known as pica. (We will look at it briefly in chapter 4.)

Unfortunately, we cannot have recourse to a straightforward eating manual, since our eating needs are all unique. The variables that affect our nutritional needs include our appetites, the efficiency of our digestive systems, our body build, DNA, brain chemistry and structure, metabolic rate, allergies, taste buds, religious customs, activities and their energy demands, cultural norms and food availability and affordability, to mention just a few.

Ask yourself these simple questions:

1. How does your appetite differ from other family members, friends and colleagues, and what do you think the reasons are for this disparity?

32

2. Does your appetite vary depending upon what you are doing or how you are feeling physically?

3. Is your appetite the same in winter as it is in summer?

4. What impact do feelings have on your food intake, such as feeling happy, angry, anxious or sad?

The challenge of choice

Added to this mix, in the Western world we now live with such a wide variety of food types, which are made available regardless of the season, 24 hours a day, seven days a week. This in itself creates further problems, since psychological studies reveal that excessive choice is a major stressor.

Coupled with the sheer expanse of available options, we are further harassed by the constant bombardment of advertising promotions from the food industry, extolling the virtues of this or that as the 'healthy choice'. We live in a world of permanent transmissions about food, which are full of endless contradictions about the benefits or dangers of low-carb diets, high-protein diets and every kind of diet under the sun.

In short, many of us are utterly confused as to what we *should* be eating for the best health. Just imagine what it would be like if the advertising of food products was banned from TV commercials, magazines, newspapers and online. How different would the contents of your fridge look?

Can we really believe that people in charge of these huge revenue streams always have the consumers' best interests at heart? One would have to be very naive indeed not to suspect that at best there is some degree of manipulation going on, which might well not be to our advantage.

Whether through advertising or through the media, we are also now frequently lectured on the importance of consuming so-called superfoods. These superfoods, such as expensive exotic berries, allegedly possesses miraculous qualities. They can apparently snaffle up free radicals in our bodies, endow us with boundless energy, halt the aging process, increase our intelligence, free us from depression and enhance our sexual libido.

I'm not saying that these superfoods do not have some beneficial qualities, as do most foods. However, the exaggeration and hype accompanying these outlandish claims lulls people into a false sense of security and may ironically lead to a less balanced diet, as they believe that the heralded superfood can meet all their bodily requirements and act as a panacea for all ills.

THINK ABOUT IT How much better would your relationship with food be if you could stop being indoctrinated by all the sales talk concerning detoxing, probiotics, antioxidants, macrobiotic, biodynamic and so on? There are many people in less modernized parts of the world who are living a perfectly healthy existence without all these scientific accoutrements at their disposal. The focus should always be on healthy eating and a healthy relationship with food, not on fads and pseudoscience.

On the other end of the spectrum from the health food racket, we are also frequently offered incentives to buy and eat more than we need. We are urged to 'go large' for a few extra pence, or are tempted by the ubiquitous BOGOFs (buy-one-get-one-free offers). Deals of every description abound, such as packets of crisps being randomly thrown in with a healthy wholemeal sandwich and bottle of water!

This marketing creep is incessant and has definitely made consumers less discerning, as few can say no to a freebie! Sadly, purchasing what we don't need has often led to either overconsumption or greater food wastage, neither of which are happy results.

Given the amount of information out there, in theory we should be more educated and food savvy today. However, we are definitely going wrong somewhere, as obesity rates soar, along with the concomitant medical complications, such as the increased incidence of diabetes, osteoarthritis and heart disease.

Mexico, the US, Australia and New Zealand are among the most obese nations in the world, but the UK is also climbing up the ranks. It is as though the best efforts of the Department of Health in promoting five portions of fruit and vegetables a day, no more than fourteen units of alcohol per week for women and 21 units for men, and the recommended intakes of salt, sugar and fish are falling on deaf ears.

Perhaps the problem is information overload and too much choice. I remember with a degree of nostalgia the meals of my childhood, when one could tell with a high degree of accuracy the day of the week depending on what dinner was served that evening.

As well as the certainty of the bill of fare on offer, we also knew that it would be offered regularly: three square meals a day consisting of breakfast, lunch and dinner. Endless grazing was not an option before the advent of fast food outlets, microwaves and convenience foods. The odd packet of crisps or biscuits along with a few sweets would be seen as an occasional treat for most youngsters of yesteryear, not part of their daily diet.

I write all this 'good old days' stuff with my tongue slightly in cheek, since actually in many ways we are better off food-wise now than we were 40 years ago. Nonetheless, many children, and adults for that matter, now expect snacks on a regular daily basis and would feel short-changed were they to have to do without. Today we rejoice in 'ready meals', which makes the skill of being able to cook largely redundant for many people. This comes at a nutritional cost since we are not in control of the extra salt, sugar and other additives that are generously included to enhance the taste and longevity of the dish. The way we eat now has damaged our relationship with food twice over: it contributes to the obesity epidemic, and it means we don't have the relationship with food that comes from cooking wholesome meals from scratch.

TRY IT NOW! Try asking people from different generations about how their eating patterns have evolved over the years. I am sure that you will find vast differences, particularly in older generations, with regard to the variety of food eaten as well as changes in the quantity and frequency of consumption. Do you eat differently now to how you did as a child?

Does the media influence problem eating?

It's easy to blame the media and the current culture of size zero models, employed to show off clothes to their greatest aesthetic advantage, as the cause of problematic eating. While they cannot be held exclusively responsible, the diet, cosmetic and fashion industries all without doubt aggravate the problem in susceptible individuals.

There was an interesting study in Fiji a few years ago that revealed how the advent of television in the mainland coincided with the emergence of eating disorders, which had been previously unheard of among the population. In a country where skinniness was traditionally viewed negatively, some young girls now aspired to emulate the thin celebrities whose images appeared on the television screen.

The study showed that many of the young people expressed extreme dismay about their body image and yearned to be thinner. Some of the girls had resorted to self-induced vomiting in an attempt to decrease their weight. As you will see in the following chapters, there are many factors in the mix, which can explain why one person may fall prey to an eating disorder while another may escape unscathed.

To summarize, there are four main categories of causes for problem eating:

1. **Genetics, hormones and chemicals:** A number of studies have shown a genetic link in the development of eating disorders. As well as genes, brain chemicals and hormones – particularly in females going through puberty – have been shown to play a causal role in eating disorder development.

2. **Disposition, environment and nurture:** An individual's mental health status will also play a part in their susceptibility to problem eating. Pre-existing conditions such as depression, anxiety, low self-worth, poor body image and feelings of hopelessness and helplessness can make an individual more vulnerable to problem eating. If family members already suffer from problem eating or aspire to look a certain way and advocate dieting, then this can also have an influence on an impressionable youngster and may trigger the onset of problem eating.

3. **Life events and experiences:** Some studies show that the development of an eating disorder can be connected to negative self-consciousness resulting from a shaming incident. Other studies have shown that

powerful negative feelings surrounding a stressful event in a person's life can trigger an eating disorder. This can be something obvious like sexual abuse, being bullied or life changes, or something more elusive such as envy of a sibling.

4. **Society, culture and socio-economic factors:** Culture clearly plays a causal role, particularly in societies where physical appearance is hugely valued. If the cultural ideal is for being either under- or overweight then this will be reflected in the self-esteem of members of that society. Socio-economic factors, such as famine or an abundance of food, affluence or poverty, can also play a role in the development of eating disorders.

 There is no single cause of problem eating. It is a complex combination of genetic, physiological, environmental, psychobiological and socio-economic factors.

4. History of problem eating

There is nothing new under the sun
Ecclesiastes 1:4–11

In this chapter I will give an overview of the history of problem eating and also briefly include all of the eating disorders listed in the *Diagnostic and Statistical Manual of Mental Disorders, Fifth Edition* (*DSM-5*), which is currently used as the universal authority for psychiatric diagnosis. Due to the limitation of space, it is not possible to discuss all eight of the eating disorder categories in detail, so I apologize in advance to any reader who may be concerned about one of the less common eating disorder conditions. But by including the diagnostic criteria, you will at least be able to recognize the symptoms and decide if you need to seek professional support by contacting your GP.

Problem eating is not a new phenomenon

Descriptions of difficult or unusual relationships with food can be found in ancient Persian, Chinese and Egyptian scrolls and hieroglyphics. Negative behaviours, such as purging and self-starvation are not new inventions; their incidence in populations varies in accordance with cultural and economic factors, among a host of other variables.

There are descriptions from the Hellenistic era that mention religious fasting leading to what we now term the illness of anorexia. It is important to note that although more evidence exists of females suffering from the various disorders throughout history, there is also clear evidence that males did not escape the clutches of these psychiatric afflictions.

Anorexia mirabilis

In the Middle Ages, a phenomenon known as *anorexia mirabilis* (miraculous absence of appetite) or 'holy anorexia' was in fashion among Catholic women as a means of demonstrating their purity and holiness. One of the most famous of these women was Saint Catherine of Siena, who lived in the 14th century and showed her devotion to Christ through celibacy and fasting.

Saint Catherine of Siena purged any food that she was made to eat by pushing twigs down her throat to make herself vomit. She died prematurely at the age of 33 as a result of starvation.

These sufferers believed that to survive without food showed that the spirit was more important than the body. By achieving this higher plane of spirituality, these deeply religious women were deemed to be closer to God. The women also pursued many other forms of penance and self-mortification to show evidence of their piety and humility, such as wearing hairshirts and performing self-flagellation.

Other notable historical figures believed to have suffered from anorexia are Saint Hedwig of Silesia (who, for the benefit of younger readers, was a duchess, not an owl), Mary Queen of Scots, Joan of Arc, Mary Tudor and Catherine of Aragon.

 There is a distinct difference between the motivation of the sufferers of anorexia mirabilis and today's anorexia nervosa sufferers – the former used fasting as a means of communicating with Christ and the latter are troubled by body image and underlying emotional problems. However, the common thread between the two forms of anorexia is the sufferer's perception that they are exercising self-discipline, which in turn creates a sense of personal control.

Thwarting the survival instinct

Although earlier motivations for anorexia may have been different from today's, both forms of anorexia lead, para-doxically, to the inevitable lack of personal volition and real control. This is because the self-imposed starvation causes the brain to malfunction and sufferers can no longer protect their own survival.

It is ironic that a quest intended to demonstrate self-discipline and autonomy leads to the sufferer's mind falling under the command of the eating disorder voice, with its insatiable desire for further weight loss, even if this ulti-mately results in death.

Early evidence of bulimia

Many people believe that bulimia first emerged in ancient Rome, with affluent Romans using a 'vomitorium' at banquets so that they could eat far more rich food than would otherwise be possible. In fact, a vomitorium was actually a passage used for easy egress from seats in an amphitheatre and not a place in which one could conveniently deposit one's lunch or dinner.

However, there is reliable evidence from the Middle Ages that wealthy people would vomit to enable themselves to eat more. Feasts and banquets in those days consisted of up to six courses. Courses would include vast quantities of goslings, rabbits, roe-deer, sturgeon, peacocks, swans, stuffed capons and wild boar and generous helpings of pastries and jellies of every description. One can appreciate the difficulty in accommodating such a bill of fare at one sitting, though clearly the obvious solution is to simply eat less.

Anorexia nervosa

It was Queen Victoria's personal physician, Sir William Gull, who first coined the term anorexia nervosa (nervous absence of appetite) having previously described it as 'anorexia hysterica'.

This change in name came about because the previously used term, 'hysterica', was reserved exclusively for women! Due to the fact that males also suffered from anorexia, it was felt that the term 'nervosa' would be more applicable.

Still, the illness scarcely featured in the general public's awareness until the second half of the 20th century. The publication of Hilde Bruch's book *The Golden Cage: The Enigma of Anorexia Nervosa* in 1978 and the death of the singer Karen Carpenter in 1983 at the age of 32 catapulted the condition into the public arena. At this point many other famous sufferers came forward, escalating the public's interest in what, in previous decades, had been dubbed a 'rich white girls' disease'.

Bulimia

Though the term had been around for a while, I believe it was Princess Diana's confession in the early 1990s that she suffered from bulimia that brought the condition to wider attention. This resulted in an avalanche of hidden sufferers coming out of the closet to seek help for this disabling illness.

Unlike anorexia, where the ravages of the disease are clearly visible, many people who suffer from bulimia can keep their problem hidden. This is because they are often able to maintain a normal weight and are therefore not readily identifiable. However, this does not mean that their psychological suffering or physical deterioration is any less acute than in those whose condition is visibly evident.

Binge eating disorder (BED)

There is scant historical evidence for binge eating disorder, also known as compulsive eating disorder. This is largely due to the fact that rather than being identified as a psychological or mental health problem, akin to addiction, in the past it was often erroneously simply attributed to greed.

Binge eating disorder is when a person repeatedly eats significantly more than what would be considered a normal amount of food within a limited time frame, and feels out of control while doing so.

In 1959, professor of psychiatry Albert Stunkard highlighted the phenomenon of binge eating and called it 'binge eating syndrome'. But it was not until as recently as 1992 that the term 'binge eating disorder' was coined. This condition was not seen as a separate category of eating disorder, and in the previous edition of the *Diagnostic and Statistical Manual of Mental Disorders – DSM-4 –* came under the group known as 'eating disorders not otherwise specified'. It wasn't until as late as 2013 that binge eating disorder was considered a distinct disorder in its own right. Thankfully, by having this recognition it is more likely that the sufferer will receive help: a step in the right direction.

Obesity

By and large, obesity, one of the potential consequences of binge eating disorder, appears to have not been overly prevalent in the past. Where it did occur, it was clearly the preserve of the aristocracy, as the poor working man and woman would not have been able to afford an excess of food.

Today, binge eating disorder is overwhelmingly the most common of the eating disorders for both males and females and is rising in many populations. Alarmingly, young children are falling prey to this disorder, as can be seen by the relatively recent rise of overweight and obese young-sters. Although a significant number of overweight people suffer from binge eating disorder, it is important to note that not all of them do.

Pica disorder

As mentioned earlier, pica disorder refers to the ingestion of non-food substances. It is difficult to trace the history of the disorder with accuracy, since it was frequently seen as a symptom of other disorders. Further confusion arises with regard to diagnosis of pica disorder because of cul-tural norms differing within various societies. Thus, identical eating practices would be deemed normal within one popu-lation and pathological in another – for example, in parts of Africa it is common for pregnant woman to eat clay, but in the UK that would be considered unusual behaviour.

Geophagia

Geophagia is the ingestion of earthy substances such as clay, soil and chalk. The practice of clay ingestion is still popular in some cultures, where it is used as a form of medication, delivering vari-ous nutrients, such as phosphorus and sulphur, from the soil. In these circumstances it would not be diagnosed as pica disorder.

Pica

One of the earliest examples of pica is the Christian mystic Angela of Foligno, who in the 13th century managed to live to the age of 61 on very little food, supplemented with non-nutritious matter such as lice, scabs and the pus from the sores of the sick and dying. She was revered for these practices, which were seen as the antithesis of four of the seven cardinal sins: gluttony, greed, pride and lust.

Rumination disorder

Rumination refers to the involuntary regurgitation of food. Rumination is normal within certain animal species, such as giraffes and cows, and is known as chewing the cud, but it is considered pathological in humans and other animal populations such as gorillas where it has also been observed.

Well-documented accounts of rumination include a patient of an Italian anatomist in 1618 who suffered from what was then known as 'rumination syndrome'. Much later we have an account of a Mauritian physiologist, Charles Edouard Brown-Sequard, who in the mid-19th century conducted an experiment upon himself to discover the response of stomach acid to different food types. By swallowing food attached to sponges and strings, he inadvertently trained himself to regurgitate food without the need of mechanical assistance; rumination became habitual and no longer under voluntary control.

Rumination disorder is most prevalent in young children and people suffering from cognitive disabilities. A cognitively healthy adult who appears to have this issue may in fact have a physical problem. Rumination disorder can adversely affect normal functioning and has been linked with depression.

Avoidant/restrictive food intake disorder (ARFID)

This is a disorder in which the limitation of food intake is *not* connected with any concerns around weight and shape. It was previously known as 'selective eating disorder' (SED) and occurs most often during childhood. This is usually only a phase, which children overcome naturally as they mature and does not require the need for medical intervention. However, a number of sufferers carry this disorder into their adult lives.

An ARFID sufferer might refuse to consume whole food groups such as vegetables and fruit. Alternatively, their choices may be based purely on the food's properties such as colour, texture, whether it is hot, cold, soft, chewy, crunchy, liquid or solid. Sufferers of ARFID will be very wary about trying out any new foods and will restrict themselves to what they regard as 'safe' foods. This anxiety will naturally impair the quality of their social life to varying degrees. When eating foods that they regard as 'unsafe' the sufferer may gag, retch or vomit, which will cause them enormous distress and reinforce their reticence in experimenting further with new types of food.

The disorder is only diagnosed if it is debilitating, causing at least one of the following: nutritional deficiency; severe weight loss; inhibition of social functioning; or the sufferer becoming dependent on nutritional supplements for survival. This disorder is frequently found in people suffering from autism and obsessive-compulsive disorder.

Other specified feeding or eating disorder (OSFED)

For the sake of completeness it is worth mentioning 'other specified feeding or eating disorders', which is a newly created category in the *DSM-5*. This category basically covers any eating behaviour which results in clinically significant distress and impairment in areas of functioning, but does not quite meet the strict diagnostic criteria of the various other eating disorders we have discussed. Often these behaviours are referred to as 'atypical'.

 Despite not meeting the full diagnostic criteria of other eating disorders, these atypical disorders can be just as dangerous and may still require medical intervention.

An OSFED sufferer will experience most of the features of a fully diagnosed eating disorder. For example, in the case of anorexia, a sufferer might have ticked every other criteria but still weigh a healthy amount, despite severe weight loss. Such a sufferer could not be diagnosed with anorexia under the current system, and would instead be diagnosed with an OSFED. Night eating syndrome and purging disorder are also located in the OSFED category.

Unspecified feeding or eating disorder (UFED)

This final category, again newly created in the *DSM-5*, is a catch-all grouping for any other forms of eating behaviours that cause clinically significant distress and impairment of functioning, but where there is insufficient information available to diagnose it as one of the main disorders.

New forms of problem eating

The following disorders are not classified as eating disorders, but have been increasing in prevalence in recent years and warrant mentioning:

Orthorexia nervosa (ON)

A person suffering from orthorexia nervosa is pathologically preoccupied with healthy eating to the extent that it materially interferes with their life. Dr Steven Bratman coined the term 'orthorexia' from the Greek word *ortho*, meaning 'correct'. The sufferer becomes obsessive about righteous eating, avoiding what they perceive as unhealthy foods, for example those containing additives.

This extreme rigidity of food selection not only interferes with the sufferer's ability to socialize, but in extreme cases has proved fatal. In the pursuit of purity, many foods become proscribed, resulting in an inadequate diet, which can lead to malnutrition and death. Although on the surface this fixation on 'healthy' eating may not appear to have a mental health component, this is far from the case. It is often linked to the sufferer being phobic about ill health or having an overriding desire for control in order to increase self-esteem.

Bigorexia

Bigorexia is a form of muscle dysmorphia where the individual becomes obsessive-compulsive about building up their physique in a quest for perfection. This will not only involve excessive body-building exercises in the gym but will also have an impact on the sufferer's diet. It affects both men and women but is more common in men.

Sufferers of bigorexia will eat a low-fat, high protein diet combined with excessive amounts of food supplements. Their mental health suffers since their body perception becomes increasingly distorted; they work out even when injured or ill and some resort to steroid abuse. The intense workout regimes interfere with both their social and work life and some sufferers have become suicidal as the psychological toll of the dysmorphia becomes unbearable.

Body dysmorphia is when an individual becomes pathologically obsessed about the way they look and has a distorted perception of their own body. Some people may fixate on the shape of their nose or the size of a scar and exaggerate this perceived defect out of all proportion. Someone suffering from anorexia will see themself as fat when they are in fact emaciated. It is also known as the imagined ugliness disease since it bears no resemblance to objective reality.

Drunkorexia

Unlike bigorexia, drunkorexia predominantly affects females. Drunkorexia is linked to body image and weight and is an unhealthy attempt to reduce calorie intake while still being able to live the 'good life'. Sufferers skip meals so that their precious calorie intake can be reserved for alcohol, enabling them to be party animals.

The dangers of this form of behaviour are substantial in the long term, since it increases the risk of liver disease, dementia and diabetes. The short-term consequences are also significant in that excessive alcohol intake on an empty stomach increases intoxication levels and lowers inhibitions, which can lead to dangerous risk-taking behaviour. In the medium term, drunkorexia increases the chances of the sufferer becoming an alcoholic and/or developing a serious eating disorder.

Pregorexia

Pregorexia is the term used for pregnant women who have a terror of pregnancy-related weight gain. It should go without saying that this is an exclusively female problem! Sufferers of pregorexia mirror the behaviour of sufferers of anorexia in that they will restrict their calorie intake and exercise compulsively. Pregorexia may also be linked to a desire to exude an aura of control and purity as a reaction to the messiness of childbirth.

This behaviour can have very severe consequences for both the mother and the unborn child, not least pregnancy complications and premature childbirth. It is more prevalent in women who have suffered physical abuse, rape or other stressful events. A genetic predisposition has been identified, and the impact of chemical and hormonal imbalances have also been suggested as potential causes for the development of pregorexia.

5. Anorexia nervosa

I. UNDERSTANDING ANOREXIA

*An emotional disorder characterized by an obsessive
desire to lose weight by refusing to eat*
Oxford Dictionary

Not loss of appetite but control of appetite

The term 'anorexia' originates from the Greek words *an*,
meaning 'without', and *orexis*, meaning 'appetite'. However,
in the case of anorexia nervosa (literally, anorexia of nervous origins), it is not that the sufferer is without appetite,
but that they try to *control* their appetite. Anorexia is a very
serious psychological illness, which typically develops during adolescence but may have a much earlier or later onset.
It affects both males and females, although female sufferers
are more prevalent.

This disorder is usually triggered by low self-esteem and
an inability to cope with emotions and worries. The irony
of the disease is that it frequently appears to target high
achievers with perfectionist tendencies. One would have
instinctively expected this demographic to have high self-
esteem, based on their innate abilities and achievements.
However, sufferers do not focus on their talents but rather
scrutinize their faults. Rather than rejoicing in achieving
95 per cent they will worry about the missing 5 per cent.

People who suffer from anorexia tend to pay great attention to detail and are analytical and very self-critical. They are usually very sensitive to criticism, hyper-vigilant to non-verbal communication and feel very threatened by change. Their typical disposition is the antithesis of what we term 'laid back'. Being relaxed and easy-going are alien concepts to those who are susceptible to this illness. Instead, they gravitate towards neatness, privacy, predictability and self-denial, since it makes them feel safe and in control. There is an abundance of scientific evidence which shows that sufferers of this disease have a marked propensity to inflate the negatives and minimize the positives in their lives. They are remarkably unforgiving of their own shortcomings.

A way of managing emotional difficulties

It is important to recognize that there are many reasons why people find themselves travelling down the road which leads to anorexia. It is not always about wanting to be skinny and model-like. Equally, many sufferers of anorexia are not trying to cling on to their childhood by maintaining child-like figures in order to avoid the responsibilities that accompany adulthood.

For some, using starvation as a means of halting puberty might well be an attempt to ward off sexual advances from others, particularly if they have experienced previous abuse. For others, anorexia comes about as the result of a simple desire to vanish, since they are consumed with self-hatred and feel worthless and undeserving. Each sufferer of anorexia is totally unique and it is unhelpful to pigeonhole them and make assumptions about why they have contracted this illness.

What does restriction of food intake achieve for the sufferer?

The sufferer sees appetite control and weight loss as a means of making themselves feel more valued and worthy. They labour under the erroneous belief that if only they were thinner they might achieve the following results:

1. They would take up less space and vanish

2. They would become more attractive and therefore happier

3. They would become more accepted and admired by others due to their ability to exercise self-discipline and restraint.

Sadly, the restriction of food intake gains its own momentum and rapidly falls outside of conscious control and choice. This is where the real problems start and the internal anorexic voice takes command.

 Sometimes when food restriction begins, friends and family initially find this slimmer version of the sufferer a positive achievement – if, for example, the person looks more toned after losing a few excessive pounds. The compliments garnered in the early stages of weight loss may serve to reinforce the illness.

By concentrating on their physical being, an individual can try to ignore their emotional concerns. To become obsessed with food intake and hunger pangs is very painful, but nonetheless it is a distraction from having to negotiate the often even more painful internal emotions which the sufferer is trying to avoid. By focusing on starving they become numb to emotional pain.

This obsession with and fragmentation of the sufferer's self-image means that all the other important qualities and achievements of the individual become subsumed and count for little compared to the inordinate emphasis they place on their physical being. Incrementally, and in some cases very rapidly, the sufferer establishes their sense of worth based purely on their weight and body shape.

Qualities and talents such as kindness, loyalty to friends, intellectual ability, honesty, musical talents and sporting abilities increasingly count for nothing if the scales do not confirm further weight loss. The person suffering from anorexia no longer sees themselves holistically, as a complex human being composed of strengths and weaknesses. Instead, weight and clothing size become the first and foremost barometers of value and worth.

Mental illness and the erosion of autonomy

In a nutshell, what starts off as the dog wagging the tail rapidly turns into the tail wagging the dog. By this I mean that as the effects of starvation take hold, the individual loses their ability to make healthy choices. The sufferer falls under the thrall of the illness as it takes its course, and the more ensconced anorexia becomes, the less real control the individual possesses, a phenomenon I term 'volition attrition'.

 Volition means the ability to use your will to make rational decisions, and attrition means a reduction in strength. So the term **volition attrition** refers to that fact that as the disease progresses and the sufferer becomes weaker, they become less and less able to make a rational assessment of their condition. This is part of the reason the disease is able to take hold and escalate so quickly.

What was initially intended as a means of gaining a sense of worthiness and control through the exercise of self-discipline and weight reduction can rapidly flip, and the sufferer can lose all real autonomy and become a slave to the anorexic voice in their head.

Those who are close to the sufferer will look on with bewilderment as they see the person they love and cherish not only diminish in size but change in personality too.

The sooner this illness is identified and treated, the better the prognosis. Later in this chapter I will discuss the signs and symptoms to look out for if you suspect you or someone you know may be suffering from anorexia.

 Early detection is crucial. It is imperative to try to arrest the disorder at the earliest opportunity, before the physical and psychological decline has taken its toll on the body and mind.

The anorexic voice

The anorexic voice in the sufferer's head is an imposter who poses as a friend and ally. Each and every day the sufferer, although exhausted due to malnutrition, will relentlessly count calories, obsess about food and strive to lose weight. Yet as soon as one weight target is achieved, the goal posts change and the anorexic voice sets yet another weight-loss challenge. This vicious cycle builds its own momentum, and the enthralled sufferer becomes increasingly weak and powerless as the disease becomes more powerful. The anorexic voice will never be satisfied, no matter how ill and underweight the sufferer may become. In essence, a form of internal Stockholm syndrome takes place between the sufferer and the destructive anorexic voice that has taken up residence in the sufferer's head, whereby the sufferer begins to sympathize with the destructive voice holding them captive.

It can also be seen as analogous to battered-person syndrome, where the victim remains loyal to their violent spouse and refuses to leave them. They irrationally argue that they must have provoked their partner and deserve the beating. They even convince themself that jealous rages and physical violence meted out on them are simply demonstrations of how passionately their spouse loves them.

In the same way that we struggle to understand why the abused spouse does not leave the bullying partner, a sufferer of anorexia does not evict the anorexic voice no matter how cruel and demanding it is. Often, the sufferer's sense of unworthiness makes them feel they deserve punishment, and the pain they consequently inflict is viewed as a form of penance.

Secrecy and social isolation

The course of the illness leads to increasing secretiveness, which tends to isolate the sufferer from their friends and family. The sufferer will try to avoid all social gatherings where food is involved in a bid to comply with the anorexic voice's demands. As the impact of the illness advances, distorted thinking becomes the norm and the sufferer may perceive the justified concerns of those around them as unrealistic and a ploy to make them fat. Anorexia eventually becomes the sufferer's only 'friend' and true friends are pushed aside or treated with contempt and suspicion.

Calm communication is essential

The two examples of the hostage and the battered person are extremely valuable in enabling us to understand how someone we love can behave in such a counter-intuitive manner. Furthermore, we can learn from these examples how to help the sufferer constructively.

In the same way that the skilled negotiator tries not to inflame the situation by verbally attacking the captor or denouncing the bullying spouse, so, too, the carer must focus on achieving calm communication with the sufferer of anorexia. The key to recovery lies in empowering the sufferer, which can only happen if they don't perceive their relationship with those who are trying to care for them as hostile and threatening.

Distorted thinking and lying

It is very difficult for those who love and care for a person caught up in the throes of this mental illness to understand their distorted form of thinking. The sufferer will insist – and believe – that they are overweight, when clearly they are malnourished and emaciated.

Frequently, the previously truthful sufferer may resort to telling their family lies, such as saying that they have already eaten when they have not or that they are going to watch a film with a friend, when in fact they are about to do a strenuous workout at the gym. Just like the distorted thinking described earlier, lying and deviousness are also recognized aspects of the disorder and should be understood in this context as not being deliberate choices.

As we will explore later in the book, it is a hopeless quest to try to argue rationally with a person suffering from anorexia about the health risks connected with inadequate nutrition and purging behaviours. The voice in their head will reward them when the scales show further weight loss and punish them for not trying hard enough if weight is gained or stabilized.

Although it is terribly difficult to resist imploring and begging your friend, child or partner to see how they are damaging themself, you can only help the sufferer to defeat the parasitic voice by keeping communication between you and them as calm and relaxed as possible. The more we denigrate the disease and urge the sufferer to act in a sane manner and start eating properly, the more resistance we will encounter.

Anorexia
Sub-type: Restricting type

Fifteen-year-old Joost's parents had been working in the United Kingdom for two years when his father was transferred to a temporary post in Africa. Believing that it was in Joost's best interest that he remain in the British education system until he had completed his GCSEs, his parents enrolled him in an all-boys boarding school.

Most of the boys in his year group had already been at the school for two years and friendship groups had been firmly established. Although Joost was not bullied, he found it difficult to settle and suffered from acute homesickness. Joost understood at an intellectual level that his father needed to accept the promotion, but nonetheless felt deserted by his family and sorely missed his younger sisters.

Having been a day-boy in his previous school, Joost found the restrictions on his liberty irksome and he experienced great difficulty in conforming to the school's traditions. Sharing a dormitory and the consequent lack of privacy made Joost feel regimented and out of control. He resented the rules about lights out at bedtime, no leisure pursuits until prep was completed and the mandatory requirement that he must join several after-school clubs.

The only areas in which he felt that he could exercise some control over his life were during the little free time he had, which he dedicated to his love of music and at mealtimes, where a self-service cafeteria offered a wide range of choices. Joost soon became aware that since boys wandered into the cafeteria at different times, nobody appeared to monitor what they ate, or even whether they attended at all. Joost soon got into the habit of skipping meals altogether, and when he did eat, it was only a few items from the salad bar.

Not being of a sporty disposition and disinclined to try to make friends, Joost spent his free time in solitary occupation in the music centre. He spent many lonely hours in total isolation within the individual cubicles, practising the piano. He spent his Christmas holidays with relatives in Holland. They noticed his thinness but put it down to a growth spurt, as he had also gained considerable height since they had last seen him. It was not until the Easter holidays, when Joost's family returned to the UK for two months' leave, that the extent of Joost's weight loss became apparent.

Joost did not return to his boarding school for the summer term and his mother and sisters stayed behind in the UK, while his father returned to Africa to complete the rest of his contract. Despite returning to day school and being reunited with his family, Joost was unable to shake off his eating disorder. A long twelve-year battle with anorexia ensued in which Joost received various forms of treatment, some of which appeared to succeed for several months before he relapsed.

Joost has now been free of anorexia for seven years. The turning point for his long-term recovery was the result of a six-month stay in a private clinic dedicated to helping people recover from eating disorders. Since leaving the clinic, Joost has maintained a healthy BMI and actually enjoys dining out with his wife.

II. PRACTICAL IDEAS
FOR UNDERSTANDING ANOREXIA

I hate and love. And why, perhaps you'll ask.
I don't know: but I feel, and I'm tormented.
Catullus

Ambivalence and anorexia – a love/hate relationship
My colleague, clinical psychologist Dr Charlotte Wing, introduced me to the following exercise, which will help you to understand the ambivalence which accompanies an eating disorder. By answering the following questions, you will gain an insight into the dilemmas faced by someone suffering from anorexia.

Find someone with whom you can do this exercise. It could be a friend or colleague. I have used this exercise with parents and partners of sufferers and they have been astounded by its impact in helping them to recognize the complexity of the love/hate relationship their child or partner has with their disorder.

Part one
- Who do you most care about/love?

- What is it about them that you love?

- What do they do that makes you feel that love for them?

Part two

- Who do you most care about/love?

- What is it about them that irritates, annoys or angers you?

- What do they do that makes you feel that irritation, annoyance or anger for them?

- What things do you dislike about them?

Part three

Now, hand your list of 'dislikes' to your partner, and hold only your 'loves'. Your partner's job is to try to convince you to leave this person, based on the negative qualities you've listed about them. Give them three minutes, see how you feel, and then swap roles and do the exercise the other way round.

I do not know who you chose as a loved one for this exercise, but let us suppose it was your partner, friend or child, who is currently suffering from an eating disorder. Maybe you produced an overwhelmingly long list of negative attributes, such as:

- They cause me constant worry about their health

- They disrupt all mealtimes

- They distress other members of the family with their tantrums

- They spoil holidays and outings with their refusal to eat in restaurants

- They lie

- They dictate what food can be purchased and methods of preparation

- They refuse to socialize and ignore their old friends

- They are self-absorbed and secretive

- Therapy can be expensive and I worry that it is depleting our savings and we may not be able to afford it indefinitely

- They cause conflict and jealousy because I devote so much time to caring for them

- They rob me of a sense of joy and fun and I neglect my own interests

- They exhaust me by the constant care I have to devote to their well-being

- My life revolves around attending hospital appointments and taking them to therapists

- I miss the carefree and loving relationship we used to have

- I am distressed to see their emaciated body shrouded in baggy clothes

- I am annoyed and embarrassed when strangers look on accusingly, as though we are not doing everything we can to try to help

- I am terrified that they might not recover

- It distresses me that they are wasting their potential by not being able to continue with their education/career.

The above list is far from comprehensive, and yet my guess is that even when the length of the negative list substantially outstrips the length of the positive list, your partner in this exercise would have been pretty unsuccessful in persuading you to leave that loved one.

But here's the twist: for a sufferer an eating disorder, the **eating disorder itself is analogous to a loved one**. This exercise mirrors very closely how someone suffering from anorexia might feel about their relationship to the eating disorder. They too are aware of the long list of negatives, which are a direct consequence of their relationship with the eating disorder. Perhaps their negatives list might look something like this:

- It has made me lose many of my friends

- I have no social life since anorexia is so time-consuming

- I hate to see my family so upset and worried about my health

- I have to lie and be secretive and I don't like being this way

- I can't continue with my favourite sports and hobbies because I am too weak

- I have no fun and am so obsessed with not putting on weight

- I feel compelled to exercise even when I am exhausted and ill

- I am jeopardizing my health

- I am always cold and tired and bruise easily

- I suffer from insomnia and hunger

- I feel fat even though people try to tell me otherwise

- I feel lonely, isolated and lack self-confidence

- My self-worth is dictated by what the scales tell me

- I feel constrained by endless food rules, which are exhausting to negotiate

- I feel guilty and a failure when I eat forbidden foods or eat too many calories

- I am a nuisance to those who love me and they would be better off if I wasn't here

- I judge myself entirely on weight and body image and all my other talents and achievements count for nothing

- I can never relax because the bully in my head keeps changing the goal posts and tells me to strive harder to reduce my weight further

- It has made me distrusting of everyone since I think that they will trick me into becoming obese so I cannot risk trying to make new friendships.

So what are the positives of anorexia in the eyes of the sufferer?

The positives you listed in the earlier exercise about the person you most care for will be many and varied. But you may be at a loss to know what sort of positives appear on the sufferer's list for their relationship with anorexia. It might look something like this:

- It makes me feel safe

- It makes me feel in control

- It wants me to be more attractive by not being fat

- It praises me when I lose weight

- It tells me that I am strong and determined when I exercise

- It provides me with an excuse for not being successful at work/relationships/passing exams because people know I am ill

- It is a constant in my life and it is mine, something special belonging exclusively to me

- It proves to the world that I have self-discipline and can control my appetite

- It helps me to feel I am invisible and take up less space in the world, so I do not attract unwanted attention

- It gives me power because others cannot separate me from it

- It gives me an identity; who would I be without it?

- It punishes me for my weaknesses by making me feel guilty, so it helps to make me a better person

- It expects perfection and high standards from me, which is good as I will be admired and become more acceptable

- It knows the real me, my shame and unworthiness, and yet never deserts me

- It helps me to shut out painful feelings and emotions by keeping me preoccupied with hunger pangs and other effects of starvation

- It is my only true and constant friend.

The important point, which I hope has been made clear by the above exercise, is that the sufferer's ambivalence about recovery is part and parcel of the disorder. Unlike a physical illness and other mental health disorders, such as depression, in which most people would be unequivocal in their desire to be cured, an eating disorder is different. It is hard to let go of something which gives you so many perceived positive as well as negative returns.

It is not dissimilar to trying to attempt to rescue someone who is clinging to a ledge of a burning building. It may
take some coaxing and building of trust before they will
be prepared to let go of the ledge and jump. It takes a
considerable leap of faith for them to believe that they will
be delivered to safety. The eating disorder, like the ledge,
offers sufferers immediate security, but is ultimately something which they will have to relinquish if they are to make
a full recovery.

Although sufferers of eating disorders would
be the first to tell you that the disorder makes
their life hell, they are nonetheless very
ambivalent about recovery. The ambivalence,
just like the lies and deceit, is an intrinsic characteristic of
the disorder. However, the positive message about ambivalence is that it signals *hope*. Enabling a sufferer of anorexia
to ultimately opt for recovery is a very delicate dance and
cannot be entered into wearing hobnail boots. Those who
apply a bullish approach are more of a liability than an asset
to ultimate recovery.

**If you are to be of any assistance in a person's recovery
from anorexia you must be prepared to:**

1. Not attempt to resolve ambivalence and contradictions,
   just accept that this is how the sufferer feels. Remember

that trying to enforce a stridently rational stance is futile. An eating disorder is by definition a distorted take on reality in which the sufferer perceives the harmful disorder as both a friend and enemy to varying degrees. With time, patience and the right support, the balance will gradually shift until the false friend is unmasked.

2. Recognize that there are two voices in the sufferer's head and direct opposition towards the anorexic voice will only promote resistance. An oblique and subtle approach is essential if you are to empower the true voice. As mentioned previously, rather than attacking the ill part of the individual, direct your efforts towards getting them back in touch with their true, multi-dimensional self. Remind them of their talents and accomplishments and the other qualities which they possess. They are so much more than their eating disorder and should never be defined in these narrow terms. (This is the reason we refer to 'sufferers of anorexia', rather than 'anorexics'.)

3. It sounds counter-intuitive, but avoid condemnation of what you perceive as negative choices made by the sufferer, since this will only make them feel bullied. A person suffering from anorexia already endures incessant internal bullying from the anorexic voice. The last thing they need is an external bully, hectoring them in a despotic fashion to further diminish their sense of autonomy. This will merely serve to compound their

sense of failure and reinforce their belief that they are a disappointment to you. Criticism will only alienate them further, which is totally counter-productive to forming a constructive relationship, an essential component if you are to be of help.

4. Recognize that progress towards recovery is seldom, if ever, linear, and do not be frustrated by setbacks, but instead help the sufferer explore their experiences in a curious and non-judgemental manner. This way they will be more open to reality and in time will garner the evidence needed to enable them to let go of the unhealthy, destructive choices that bring them distress.

5. Resist the urge to take over total control to try to fix the problem. This will result in a pyrrhic victory, and in time the sufferer will become more resistant and wary of your attempts to help. Remember, you can only be with the sufferer temporarily, whereas the anorexic voice has the upper hand and is in the sufferer's head permanently. Ultimately, unless the sufferer establishes autonomous control over their own life they will be at risk of further relapses. Empowerment of the individual is the only long-term solution.

Defeating the eating disorder voice

I have always loved the Cherokee parable below and have found it to be inspirational in helping clients to defeat the eating disorder voice. Sufferers may have become divorced from their true rational voice, which has become so muffled by the eating disorder that they need some help in turning up the volume.

'Two wolves'

One evening an old man told his grandson about a battle that goes on inside people. He said, 'My son, the battle is between two wolves inside us all. One is evil: It is anger, envy, jealousy, sorrow, regret, greed, arrogance, self-pity, guilt, resentment, inferiority, lies, false pride, superiority, and ego. The other is good: It is joy, peace, love, hope, serenity, humility, kindness, benevolence, empathy, generosity, truth, compassion and faith.'

The grandson thought about it for a minute and then asked the grandfather: 'Which wolf wins?'

The old man simply replied: 'The one that you feed the most.'

After reading this parable to the sufferer, I will introduce the notion of the 'best friend voice'. This simply involves following up harsh, irrational statements the sufferer might come out with – such as 'I am useless/disgusting/worthless' with the following: 'What do you think your best friend would say to you about that?' or 'What would you say to your best friend if he/she said those things about him/herself?'

The 'eating disorder voice' and the 'best friend voice' are analogous to the evil wolf and the good wolf in the parable above. Often clients find it difficult to treat themselves with compassion and respect, being so convinced that they are unworthy or bad. By asking them what they think their best friend, or their good wolf, would say to them, the task becomes easier, since they are forced out of their own negative frame of reference.

I find that with patience and practice the client learns to feed the good wolf, who gains in strength and power, and ignore the evil wolf, whose powers then dwindle and diminish.

 A conversation between the evil wolf and the good wolf (or the eating disorder voice and the best friend voice) might look something like this:

Evil wolf: You are greedy and weak for eating that meal.

Good wolf: It may feel that way for you at the moment, but a part of you recognizes that without nourishment you will not be able to compete in the sports that you love. Nor will you be able to concentrate on the revision you need to do in order to pass your degree.

Evil wolf: Nobody likes you; they all think that you are a failure.

Good wolf: Sometimes we may feel a little bit unlovable, but when we think about it realistically there is plenty of evidence to refute that claim. You have many friends and have been successful in your job and have many other accomplishments.

Evil wolf: You have no willpower whatsoever; you totally lack self-discipline.

Good wolf: I can understand that you are disappointed that you succumbed to another binge, but we are all human and falter from time to time. Remember that the binges have become less frequent, and you're making steady progress. You also have considerable willpower, otherwise you would never have got to grade 7 on the piano because it took hours of practice to get there.

 Think about what the negative voice in your head is telling you, and then respond with the voice of your best friend or good wolf. Remember not to argue or engage with the negative 'evil wolf' but use the constructive 'good wolf' to gently remind you of the evidence that supports another perspective.

III. DIAGNOSIS AND SYMPTOMS OF ANOREXIA

People lose weight for many different reasons, some of which we have discussed earlier. It is important to recognize that weight loss may be the result of other physical problems. Cachexia, for example, is a wasting disorder in which the individual is unable to utilize the nutrients and vitamins from the food ingested and so loses weight despite eating normally.

It is also not unusual for people who are grieving to suffer from a lack of appetite and to lose weight as a result. Depressed people are frequently neglectful about their needs and sometimes fail to cook proper meals for themselves, but this is not intended as a deliberate act to lose weight. All of these things should be investigated before a diagnosis of anorexia is given.

In line with *DSM-5*, a diagnosis of anorexia is given *only* if all three of the following criteria are met:

1. Significantly lower body weight than what would be expected for the age, sex and developmental stage of the individual. This is caused by self-induced starvation resulting in severe weight loss which compromises the individual's health.

2. Despite being significantly underweight, the individual suffers from an intense fear of gaining weight.

3. The individual suffers from a disturbance in the way that they experience their weight or shape, and this plays an overly powerful role in how they evaluate themself, or they are in denial about the dangers of their current low body weight.

Anorexia: restricting type

This is the most common type of anorexia, in which the sufferer severely restricts the number of calories they take in each day. Some individuals restrict by only eating one meal a day, while others may limit themselves to following obsessive, rigid rules such as permitting themselves to only eat one food type or colour. The other types of food will be perceived by the sufferer as 'forbidden', and they will suffer great distress if forced to eat them.

Anorexia: binge-eating or purging type

This type of anorexia occurs less frequently. As well as restricting food intake, sufferers of this type will often resort to bingeing or purging behaviours too. This is because starving oneself is difficult, and sufferers of anorexia may succumb to their appetite but then regret having eaten something. This causes them to indulge in purging, such as self-induced vomiting or misuse of diuretics, enemas and laxatives, or other inappropriate compensatory behaviours, such as over-exercising, to rid themselves of the excess calories.

Both starvation and excessive exercising alter brain chemistry and cause an increase in serotonin levels. Sufferers of anorexia become addicted to the high that this creates.

Warning signs and symptoms of anorexia

Below I have listed some of the many signs and symptoms of anorexia. Some of these symptoms do not arise in the earlier stages of the illness and only become evident once the illness has progressed. Please be aware that although some signs are both psychological and behavioural, I have only allocated them to one category to avoid repetition.

Psychological signs:

- Depression

- Suicidal ideation

- Refusal to acknowledge dangers attached to their low weight

- Distorted thinking – complaining that they are overweight when they're not

- Self-evaluation based inordinately on physical appearance

- Escalation of obsessive or ritual behaviours

- Increasing secretiveness

- Difficulty in concentrating on anything but the topic of food

- Low self-esteem and constant self-criticism

- Moodiness, irritability and inflexibility

- Engaging in black and white thinking, no in-between

- Intensification of perfectionism

- Withdrawal from relationships and increased social isolation

- Becoming indecisive, unable to meet deadlines

Physical signs:
- Weight loss

- Reduction in white blood cell count

- Anaemia, electrolyte and mineral abnormalities, zinc deficiency

- Thinning of hair

- Stomach pains

- Oedema (swelling of hands, face or feet)

- Dry skin, chapped lips, brittle fingernails and bruising

- Poor circulation, purplish looking hands and feet

- Reduced metabolism

- Feeling cold constantly or suffering from hypothermia

- Bad breath and tooth decay caused by vomiting

- Loss of teeth due to weakening of the jawbone

- Dizziness, light-headedness or fainting

- Bloating, constipation or diarrhoea

- Amenorrhoea in females (no onset or cessation of menstruation)

- Insomnia and tiredness

- Low blood pressure, slow heart rate

- Hardened skin around knuckles caused by inducing vomiting

- Impotence in men

- Growth of lanugo (downy hair) over the body and face

- Loss of libido

- Headaches

- Osteoporosis

- Reduced immune system

- Frail appearance, sunken eyes and pallid complexion

Behavioural signs:
- Repeated weighing

- Frequent checking in the mirror

- Only eating low-calorie foods and obsessive counting of calories

- Refusal or discomfort around dining in public

- Avoiding various foods

- Skipping meals

- Taking slimming pills, laxatives or diuretics

- Hiding, hoarding or throwing away food

- Obsessive reading of cookery books

- Cooking elaborate meals for others but not eating the food prepared

- Constant excuses as to why they are not eating

- Self-harm or substance abuse

- Aggressiveness when encouraged to eat 'forbidden foods'

- Cutting food up into tiny bits before swallowing

- Dissecting food to try to conceal how much has been left on the plate

- Avoiding eating with others, even at home

- Wearing baggy clothes to disguise weight loss

- Talking about food constantly

- Lying about weight

- Strict dieting

- Vanishing straight after meals to go to the loo or their room

- Pretending that they have already eaten

- Over-exercising

- Frequent measuring of body, e.g. waist or tops of thighs

- Withdrawing from interests

Anorexia
Sub-type: Binge-eating or purging type

Twenty-four-year-old Clarissa had suffered from anorexia for three years. Her illness started shortly after joining a predominantly male aeronautical engineering company. Clarissa, a very pretty girl with an attractive figure, drew unwanted attention from many of the employees. Although nothing was said overtly, their manner of interacting with her during meetings made her feel uneasy. She started to isolate herself from their stares by avoiding the company cafeteria and went without lunch. She also refused to attend any work-related social events and consequently did not become friendly with any of her colleagues.

Clarissa had moved to the area purely for employment purposes, so had no family nearby in whom she could confide her loneliness and work concerns. Clarissa quickly stopped wearing her figure-hugging clothes and started to wear shapeless outfits for work. In addition, she began to neglect feeding herself adequately, only allowing herself one small meal each day in her attempt to become invisible. Despite the meagreness of her calorie intake, she felt compelled to burn off these calories before going to bed. Each evening, although cold and suffering from fatigue, she forced herself to cycle to the local gym. On arriving at the gym, Clarissa embarked on a gruelling two-hour exercise routine, which left her exhausted and light-headed.

Over the years, despite her wearing a baggy tracksuit, her emaciated figure became apparent and caused distress to other gym users who were concerned for her welfare. As a result of these concerns, the manager of the gym approached Clarissa and asked if she could support her in seeking medical help since she was clearly underweight. Clarissa stoutly refused this offer, denying that there was a problem. Eventually the manager had no other choice than to revoke Clarissa's membership on the grounds of health and safety.

At this point Clarissa sought gym membership elsewhere but was again refused. Frustrated by this outcome, she created an improvised gym in her own home by repeatedly stepping up and down on the two bottom steps of her staircase. She followed this routine by a series of sit-ups and squats, followed by 30 minutes on a static bike in which she had invested. Although Clarissa was becoming progressively weaker and her weight dangerously low, she continued with this relentless regime until one evening she collapsed.

Fortunately, a concerned neighbour noticed that the lights had not been switched off throughout the entire night and called round to see if everything was okay. On receiving no reply, the neighbour alerted the emergency services and as a result Clarissa was swiftly hospitalized. Having undergone inpatient treatment to stabilize her precarious physical condition, Clarissa went on to receive outpatient support in the community. Clarissa is still on her path to recovery and attends weekly interpersonal psychotherapy sessions (which will be discussed in chapter 11) to help her to address the original underlying issues of her eating disorder.

6. Bulimia nervosa

I. UNDERSTANDING BULIMIA

An emotional disorder characterized by a distorted
body image and an obsessive desire to lose weight,
in which bouts of extreme overeating are followed
by fasting or self-induced vomiting or purging
Oxford Dictionary

General overview of the disorder

The word bulimia originated from the Greek words *bous*, meaning 'ox', and *limos*, meaning 'hunger' – it literally means 'the hunger of an ox'. The sufferer of bulimia oscillates between excessive overeating followed by fasting, restriction of food intake or purging.

Studies reveal that one in a hundred people in the UK suffer from this disorder, of which 10 per cent are male. Other studies, however, indicate that in recent years this figure has risen to 20 per cent of male sufferers. This could well be as a result of men in the public eye coming forward and sharing their experiences with this illness, including John Prescott and Paul Gascoigne.

Many sufferers of bulimia have other, coexisting disorders such as obsessive-compulsive disorder (OCD), anxiety disorder, post-traumatic stress disorder (PTSD) and depression. Sufferers are also at increased risk of developing alcohol or drug dependency. According to some studies, bulimia may be caused by lowered serotonin function, and there is also evidence that cultural pressures and childhood conflicts may play a key role in causation too.

As with anorexia, the development of the disorder has been linked to severe stress, physical illness, sexual abuse and other forms of trauma. Research has also revealed that there could be a genetic component, which predisposes people to developing this condition. The condition is four times more likely to occur if a close relative has suffered from it, although the jury is still out as to whether this is nature or nurture, or a combination of the two.

Dieting and bulimia

As with anorexia, the key contributor to development of this eating disorder is low self-esteem, and this sense of lack of worth makes people particularly vulnerable to feeling that they should conform to society's expectations. Sufferers often have a very poor body image, which makes them an easy target for dieting, particularly if they have been teased or bullied about their size or shape. Children who have been overweight are particularly susceptible to this illness, as are those who have experienced the death of a parent or parental separation. Dieting is often the starting point of this illness.

It is worth mentioning that some sufferers of bulimia may at some point have been sufferers of anorexia. It can also go the opposite way, with the sufferer of bulimia becoming a sufferer of anorexia. The term 'bulimarexia' is used for a sufferer who runs on a cycle of both conditions.

The typical onset of this illness is in late adolescence and early twenties, and it is much more common in females than males. It is a very hidden disorder due to the fact that sufferers, unlike those who are afflicted with anorexia, are not usually readily identifiable, being of normal weight or slightly overweight. One of the key distinguishing aspects between anorexia and bulimia is that the sufferer of bulimia is not morbidly terrified of attaining normal body weight, which is the case of someone suffering from anorexia. Bulimia is also about four times more prevalent than anorexia.

Bulimia is a very secretive illness, since sufferers are repulsed by their behaviour and go to great lengths to keep their 'sordid' habits hidden. 'Sordid' is not my expression, but one that has been used on a number of occasions by my clients who feel disgusted by their actions. For obvious reasons, this is an extremely messy disorder and can cause considerable inconvenience for other family members or housemates. Sharing a home with someone who suffers from bulimia can mean that the bathroom is often occupied and frequently loos and sinks are blocked as a result of purging behaviours. Food packaging may be stuffed under sofas and behind cushions to hide evidence of bingeing.

 Though sufferers of bulimia may not be seriously underweight, it is still an extremely serious psychiatric disorder, with many negative physical and mental side-effects.

A way of coping with difficult emotions

Just like anorexia, bulimia is used as a displacement activity to avoid handling painful and difficult emotions. The misuse of food is merely a symptom of underlying problems and the sufferer's inability to get their needs met as a consequence of their low self-esteem and possible lack of assertiveness. Bulimia frequently starts with attempts to lose weight by dieting in order to enable the individual to feel more in control and attractive by conforming to societal pressure to be slim.

Once again, the sufferer places an excessive emphasis on their physical appearance, despite the likelihood that they possess a great many qualities and skills that make them appear competent and confident to the outside world. Many people suffering from bulimia have very demanding, high-powered jobs and appear extremely outgoing and confident.

They tend to present to the outside world a veneer of composure, but underneath the surface the sufferer of bulimia dwells in uncertainty, insecurity and low self-esteem. They are desperate to gain the approval of others and fear rejection, since they are often convinced of their own inadequacy. They frequently are people-pleasers and fail to assert themselves to get their needs met.

Bingeing or gorging

When someone with bulimia tries to maintain their strict regime of dieting or fasting, they often experience extremely acute hunger, which they then assuage by binge-ing. As well as starvation, bingeing can also be triggered by tiredness, boredom, anger or loneliness. These are not dissimilar to the reasons that some people abuse alcohol.

Bingeing is the term used for when someone consumes an excessive amount of food within a short space of time and feels totally out of control while doing so. An average binge will involve the consumption of 3,000–5,000 calories in approximately an hour.

Gastric dilation and gastric rupture can happen in extreme episodes of bingeing as a result of consuming such colossal quantities of food in such a short space of time that the body can't handle it. People suffering from bulimia are also much more prone to developing peptic ulcers and pancreatitis.

When caught up in the binge phase, the sufferer shows little discernment and will often eat whatever is to hand, including un-defrosted or uncooked food and any leftovers sitting in the fridge. So intense is the compulsion to eat that some sufferers have even resorted to eating pet food or food which had been consigned to the dustbin.

Guilt, shame and embarrassment

Huge tubs of ice-cream, family-sized buckets of fried chicken and bumper packs of biscuits, crisps and nuts can be demolished in one sitting, amounting to a massive calorie count. Some sufferers have been known to consume in a single binge more than five times the recommended daily intake of calories.

As you can imagine, eating five days' worth of food in less than two hours requires a reckless level of speed and the food will scarcely be tasted. The sufferer uses the food to stuff down whatever uncomfortable feelings are welling up inside of them.

They then panic and experience considerable physical discomfort, accompanied by enormous guilt and shame as a result of their frenzied lack of restraint. They feel an overwhelming urge to get rid of the excessive calories, which compels them to resort to purging or other compensatory behaviours such as fasting or over-exercising.

 Purging is a way of getting rid of the excess calories consumed and may take different forms, such as self-induced vomiting or the misuse of enemas, laxatives or diuretics. Some sufferers take diet pills, thyroxine, amphetamines, insulin and emetics. Others indulge in **compensatory behaviours** such as over-exercising in an attempt to burn off the excessive calories.

The eating pattern of a person suffering from bulimia may be totally chaotic, consisting of a relentless cycle of bingeing and purging. However, some individuals are able to eat relatively normally when they are around other people, say within their working environment, but then fall into chaotic eating habits when alone.

Self-induced vomiting

The frequency of bingeing and purging differs between individuals, with some vomiting several times a day and others only several times a week. Generally speaking, the longer the illness progresses, the more adept the individual becomes at self-induced vomiting and the more cunning they become at hiding this habit.

It doesn't take long before the self-induced vomiting disrupts the body's ability to signal satiety. This further facilitates the bingeing phase, since the sufferer no longer has the normal signals to indicate when they are full. Someone who frequently vomits will have calluses on their hands due to pushing their fingers down their throat.

Since vomit contains gastric acid, which is highly corrosive, a sufferer's tooth enamel will wear away and result in increased sensitivity. This will be particularly painful when consuming hot or cold drinks. The teeth of sufferers often take on an unattractive yellowish hue and look very glassy.

In addition, as a consequence of sugary snacks – a popular binge choice along with high-fat foods – the sufferer will be very prone to tooth decay or caries. Vomiting can also cause the throat and oesophagus to tear or rupture. This can lead to chronic soreness and hoarseness as well as blood appearing in the vomit.

More seriously, as a consequence of vomiting, the body can become dangerously dehydrated and lacking in electrolytes. This can have a fatal impact on vital organs, in severe cases causing a heart attack or kidney failure. Electrolytes such as chloride, magnesium, potassium and sodium are needed for nerve and muscle function as well as fluid regulation, and it is critical that they are kept in balance.

Laxatives

Those who use laxatives as a means of purging need to constantly increase their dosage in order to achieve the same effects, as their body loses its ability to function normally. Many individuals who abuse laxatives cause damage to the bowel muscles, which results in bloating and permanent constipation.

Damage to the gut wall caused by laxative abuse can be so severe that the sufferer may require surgery to remove damaged sections and might need to have a colostomy bag fitted. Some laxatives contain phenolphthalein, which damages blood cell production and suppresses the functions of bone marrow.

Consumption of large quantities of laxatives causes considerable physical discomfort and may also be used by the sufferer as a means of self-harming to distract from the painful emotions they are trying to avoid dealing with. Furthermore, use of laxatives as a method of getting rid of excess calories is woefully ineffective since most have already been absorbed long before they reach the large intestine, the site where the laxative takes effect.

Diuretics

Diuretics are substances used to increase the rate of urination. The sufferer uses these substances, often in the form of pills, as a means of losing weight. They might also excessively drink tea or coffee, as these have natural diuretic properties.

As with the misuse of laxatives, this is not a successful method for losing weight since it simply deprives the body of much-needed water. The lack of water can cause disruption of the functioning of many important physiological systems in the body. This can result in complications ranging from dizziness to serious kidney damage.

A vicious cycle

Once the cycle of bingeing and purging has begun it quickly gains momentum. As a consequence of inadequate nutrition in the restrictive phase, a starvation reaction follows, which creates an irresistible urge to eat. The experience of hunger is hugely enhanced due to blood glucose levels being out of kilter. This urge to eat is so overwhelming that the need to eat becomes uncontrollable, hence the binge.

Along with the resultant metabolic imbalances caused by this behaviour, the sufferer's already fragile self-esteem is eroded further as the shame and guilt become more ingrained. The individual feels out of control and worthless as they desperately try to put their energy into keeping their weight down. Focusing on their body image then becomes all-consuming and addictive.

As a result of their unbearable negative feelings of hopelessness, indignity and self-condemnation, the sufferer tries to increase the strictness of the diet, even resorting to total fasting, but this in turn increases the cravings, as the body desperately demands food. With this obsessive preoccupation with food, the sufferer inevitably snaps and breaks the diet.

Once the diet has been broken, the sufferer, due to their tendency towards 'all or nothing' thinking, will feel that they have totally failed. The message is that they have blown it anyway by eating something which they feel they should not have consumed. Perhaps it was a 'forbidden food'. So, as the saying goes, 'in for a penny, in for a pound'. This gives them temporary justification for the binge, which is then immediately regretted.

The inevitable purging or compensatory behaviour provides an instant feeling of relief as the tension is released. This, however, is short-lived and is swiftly overtaken by feelings of self-loathing and disgust. They find themself right back at the start of the cycle, and it begins all over again.

The concept of 'forbidden food' is a recipe for disaster. No foods should be forbidden, since it only serves to set up cravings in the brain for what we are not allowed to have. One only has to look at the old biblical story of Adam and Eve to see the consequence of the forbidden apple!

If you were told by a parent or partner to never open a particular drawer in their desk, you may or may not open it, depending on your character. However, I can assure you that at the very least you will expend a fair amount of energy in suppressing your curiosity. It is just the same with 'forbidden foods': the more we deny ourselves, the more likely we are to capitulate and give in to our craving.

A much healthier approach is encapsulated in the old maxim, 'all things in moderation and moderation in all things'.

The impact of bulimia

Bulimia not only harms the individual physically, psychologically and emotionally, but also causes a number of social problems. To accommodate their embarrassing behaviours and mood swings, sufferers may start to isolate themselves and withdraw from family, friends and colleagues.

Some sufferers experience difficulty in holding down a job, since catering for their cycles of bingeing and facilitating purging is very demanding in terms of time, energy and finance. The workplace is not always conducive to these habits. Continuing in employment may become impossible, particularly if sufferers frequently absent themselves to seek out public loos in order to purge and take extensive breaks for bingeing purposes.

Some sufferers spend a copious amount of time making elaborate plans and preparations for the binge phase. Often they will travel far afield in order to not be recognized when they stock up on vast quantities of food.

Supplying enough food to accommodate the binge phase can prove expensive, and sadly many young sufferers in particular have resorted to stealing money from their family or to shoplifting to fund their habit. This is very similar to the experiences of a drug addict, the only difference being that food is a legal substance.

THINK ABOUT IT

Bulimia metaphorically reflects the chaos of the internal emotional world of the sufferer. The bulimic cycle mirrors the painful emotions and feelings which the sufferer is unable to express in a legitimate way.

For example, if the sufferer feels hatred or rage and these feelings seem too dangerous to be expressed because of the potential damage they may cause within the family, workplace or friendship group, the individual will try to suppress them or push them down by bingeing.

When the suppression becomes too unbearable and the anger builds too high, this 'explosion' is represented by the elimination or purging phase. The consequent feelings of guilt and shame, which are attached to the expression of the hatred or rage are akin to the fasting phase. This restrictive phase not only acts as a means of trying to reassert personal control but can also be felt as a way of doing penance, a form of punishment for having these bad feelings in the first place.

CASE STUDY

Bulimia
Purging type

Shaimaa had always been in tremendous awe of her older sister Gamila, who was four years her senior. Success seemed to come naturally to Gamila, and Shaimaa constantly compared herself unfavourably to her sibling. Gamila enjoyed a lucrative and interesting career as a journalist and was held in high esteem within her friendship circle.

Shaimaa's career as a country solicitor seemed unexciting in comparison. Her social life would have been almost non-existent were it not for Gamila inviting her younger sister to join her and her group of friends in London for the odd weekend.

Living in the shadow of her popular, slim and very glamorous sister, Shaimaa regarded herself as unattractive, frumpy and dull. For several years Shaimaa had resorted to strict dieting regimes only to give up after several weeks and swiftly pile back on the weight, plus a little extra.

When Gamila got engaged, Shaimaa felt both jealous and left out, since the couple spent every available opportunity exclusively in each other's company. The sparse social life that Shaimaa had previously enjoyed, by dint of her sister's invitations, came to an abrupt halt.

It was at this point that Shaimaa started to binge as a way of consoling herself during the long boring evenings, which she spent on her own. During her lunch break at work, Shaimaa would shop for her evening binge. On arriving home she would do some household chores and then settle down in front of the television set and mindlessly eat her way through that day's food purchases.

Already lacking in self-confidence and hating her physical appearance, Shaimaa became increasingly insecure and depressed as her weight steadily increased. The binges became more elaborate and intense until she could scarcely make it through the front door before devouring the contents of her shopping bags.

Feeling totally out of control and incapable of managing the binges, Shaimaa resorted to trying to make herself sick. This was initially unsuccessful, so in desperation Shaimaa started to take laxatives to try to get rid of the excess calories. But despite regularly increasing the amount of laxatives, her weight continued to increase.

Deciding that laxatives alone were not working, Shaimaa persevered with her attempts to make herself sick and eventually became adept at the practice. As the months passed Shaimaa's work began to suffer due to her obsessive preoccupation with food, which hindered her ability to concentrate. Shaimaa's physical health also started to suffer and she experienced a painfully sore throat and various stomach problems.

Feeling ashamed and full of self-loathing as the bingeing, vomiting and laxative intake escalated, the stress became so unbearable that Shaimaa started to self-harm, as a way of releasing the ever-mounting tension. Although this afforded

Shaimaa some form of short-term relief from her overwhelming feelings of despair, by temporarily dulling her intense emotions, her depression and self-hatred only intensified.

As a result of the deepening depression, Shaimaa frequently called in sick and was absent from work on a number of occasions. Hearing through the grapevine that her sister was unwell, Gamila arrived unexpectedly at Shaimaa's apartment to see how she was and disturbed her during one of her episodes of self-harming. Horrified by what she saw, a tremendous row ensued in which Gamila threatened to tell their parents unless Shaimaa agreed to go for professional help immediately.

Shaimaa eventually broke down and confided in Gamila that she had always felt boring and the ugly duckling when she compared herself to her sister. She also disclosed that she had been suffering from bulimia and depression and had on several occasions considered committing suicide. Realizing the extent of her sister's illness, Gamila encouraged Shaimaa to make an appointment with her GP.

Shaimaa had to give up her job and is currently living with her mother's widowed sister while recovering. She is still receiving treatment in the community for both the eating disorder and depression. Considerable progress has been made on both fronts and Shaimaa has managed to reduce the frequency of her binges and purges to approximately twice a week. Her laxative intake is slowly being reduced and she no longer self-harms.

Shaimaa has established an excellent relationship with

her cognitive analytic therapy practitioner, Alena (we will look more at CAT in chapter 11). As a result of this bespoke therapy, Alena has helped Shaimaa to work through her deep-seated feelings of inferiority in relation to her sister.

Having understood how her behaviour developed and was being maintained, Shaimaa now feels motivated to change her eating behaviours. The therapy has also enabled Shaimaa to recognize her lack of interest and self-fulfillment in her legal career. It is her intention, once recovered, to do some voluntary work overseas for a year, and she then plans to retrain as a social worker.

In my work with clients with bulimia I have found the following exercise to be very helpful. Make a card that you can keep in your wallet or bag containing the following instructions:

1. I promise to give myself five minutes of slow breathing before I take any further action.

2. I promise to ask myself if this is really what I want to do and I will read my list of why I don't want to continue with this behaviour, for example: I don't want to have bad breath, jeopardize my health, feel guilt and remorse, etc.

3. If I still feel out of control I can ring the numbers below to speak to a friend or a helpline. (List your friends that you can talk to and make sure that you put down several

just in case someone is unavailable. Add the helpline
numbers listed at the end of this book.)

Whenever you feel compelled to binge or purge promise
yourself that you will look at your card first.

II. DIAGNOSIS AND SYMPTOMS OF BULIMIA

In accordance with *DSM-5*, a diagnosis of bulimia is given
only if all five of the criteria below are met:

1. Repeated episodes of compulsive eating within a short
    space of time (less than two hours) of large quantities
    of food and feeling out of control while doing so. This
    is known as bingeing.

2. Repeated inappropriate compensatory behaviour to
    prevent the weight gain by trying to get rid of the food
    consumed. This is known as purging and may take the
    form of self-induced vomiting, misuse of laxatives, ene-
    mas and diuretics, or over-exercising.

3. Criteria one and two (bingeing and compensatory
    behaviour) must occur at least once a week for a mini-
    mum of three months.

4. An individual's self-evaluation is inordinately based
    upon their body shape and weight.

5. The disturbance does not occur exclusively during epi-
    sodes of anorexia.

Bulimia: purging type
Purging type refers to the sufferer engaging in self-induced vomiting or misusing diuretics, laxatives or enemas during the bulimic episode.

Bulimia: non-purging type
Non-purging type refers to sufferers who do not engage in any of the behaviours described above but do engage in other forms of inappropriate compensatory behaviours during the bulimic episode. Examples of these behaviours are excessive over-exercising or fasting.

Below are some of the warning signs and symptoms of bulimia:

Psychological signs:
- Preoccupation with body image and weight
- Mood swings, hyperactivity, irritability and depression
- Feeling out of control when eating, uncontrollable urge to eat
- Preoccupation/obsession with food
- Obsession with dieting
- Experiencing shame, guilt or disgust about eating behaviours
- Personality change

- Tremendous fear of gaining weight

- Overly emotional and anxious

- Feeling isolated, lonely and helpless

- Low self-esteem

Physical signs:
- Slow pulse, low blood pressure

- Brittle nails

- Bleeding or receding gums, mouth sores

- Calluses on knuckles due to putting fingers down the throat

- Tooth decay caused by erosion of enamel due to vomiting

- Discoloured, yellow teeth caused by exposure to stomach acids when vomiting

- Bad breath, mouth infections

- Irregular menstrual cycles

- Vision disturbances

- Neuro-muscular problems

- Heart palpitations

- Loss of mental acuity and memory

- Swollen glands in neck, face and throat causing a chipmunk-like appearance

- Dark circles and puffiness under eyes

- Low libido, infertility, miscarriages

- Cold sweats

- Mineral deficiencies

- Fatigue and lethargy

- Light-headedness, fainting

- Change in lower jaw alignment and bite

- Warm, clammy skin and poor skin condition

- Thinning hair

- Weight fluctuations but within normal range

- Sore throat, hoarseness

- Bowel problems, especially constipation

- Stomach pains, bloating, acid reflux, ruptured stomach/ oesophagus

- Swollen hands and feet

- Broken blood vessels in the eyes

- Dehydration

- Sleep problems

- Heart and kidney problems

- Muscle spasms

- Fits or convulsions

Behavioural signs:

- Binge eating in secret

- Vomiting in secret

- Reluctance to socialize

- Exercising excessively/compulsively

- Rigid dieting

- Eating at night

- Excessive food intake with no apparent weight gain

- Hiding, hoarding, stealing to purchase huge quantities of food

- Hiding laxatives and diuretics

- Planning binges

- Disappearing straight after meals to purge

- Spending considerable time in the loo

- Running the tap while in the loo to disguise the sound of vomiting

- Blocking lavatories and sinks

- Excessive use of air freshener/scent to conceal the smell of vomit

- Disappearance of food from cupboards and fridge

- Using diuretics, enemas or laxatives or saunas to sweat out water

- Running out of money due to spending on binges

- Anxious to shoo people out of the kitchen so they can prepare for binges

- Being surrounded by discarded food wrappers and packaging

- Frequently complaining about a sore throat (caused by vomiting)

- Wearing baggy clothes

- Eating in secret

- Lying about where food has gone or what has been eaten

- Denial about being hungry

- Alternating between fasting and overeating

Bulimia

Non-purging type

Jarek and his twin brother Iwan ran a very successful small business as personal fitness trainers.

During the economic recession the business was hit hard due to the sudden reduction in clients.

Both Jarek and Iwan were eventually forced to take on additional employment to supplement their income and meet their financial commitments. Iwan took on part-time work at a local garage, while Jarek secured evening shifts as a waiter in a nearby restaurant.

Having enjoyed the autonomy of being self-employed, both brothers found it difficult having to adapt to taking orders from supervisors and bosses. It was during this transition that Jarek's girlfriend called time on their three-year relationship. Jarek took this very badly and felt that his world was falling apart.

Apart from working with a handful of clients during the week, Jarek's days were largely unstructured, and he was left with plenty of spare time to ruminate over his failed relationship and struggling business. While Iwan was working at the garage, Jarek got into the habit of comfort eating.

Jarek didn't know how to express his growing anger and resentment and so began to binge on a regular basis. He would steal food from the restaurant and even bring home leftover food from customers' plates, such as half-eaten pizzas. These binges gave Jarek temporary respite from the unfairness of his situation but then having binged he suffered unbearable remorse and shame.

Conscious of the importance of a toned body in the world of fitness trainers, Jarek would immediately panic about the excess calories he had consumed. He soon fell into the pattern of following these binges with intense workouts lasting three to four hours, which left him utterly exhausted before starting his evening shifts.

Several times Jarek tried to put a stop to this cycle he had fallen into by starving himself for a couple of days at a time. He realized that the bingeing and over-exercising was jeopardizing his work in the restaurant. The acute tiredness caused him to be irritable and he had been warned about his rudeness towards customers. His brain was foggy, and he had also made frequent mistakes with muddling up orders and giving incorrect change to customers.

But the days of total food deprivation only served to inflame the intensity of the binges when the self-starvation became unbearable. This in turn ramped up the need for even more hours of excessive exercising.

This state of affairs persisted for several months, and it was not until Jarek collapsed during one of his training sessions with a client that he truly acknowledged the damage he was doing to himself. Jarek sought the advice of his cousin, a medical student, who put him in touch with a self-help group for people suffering from eating disorders. By attending the group, Jarek was made aware of the benefits of meditation and massage (which are discussed in chapter 13) and, having incorporated these practices into his weekly routine, found he felt much less agitated and tense.

His cousin also recommended a number of books about eating disorders and gave him a helpline telephone number, which proved to be invaluable when Jarek felt the urge to binge. It took almost a year for Jarek to feel that he was no longer in danger of relapsing into bingeing behaviour. Jarek's health and self-confidence has improved greatly, and the twins' personal fitness training business is also showing signs of recovery as the recession eases.

7. Binge eating disorder

I. UNDERSTANDING BINGE EATING DISORDER

The consumption of large quantities of food in a short period of time, typically as part of an eating disorder
Oxford Dictionary

General overview of the disorder

Binge eating disorder (BED) is a form of compulsive overeating and is the most prevalent of all eating disorders. It is a form of addiction to food in which individuals feel incapable of restraining themselves from eating. Like the previous eating disorders discussed, the main underlying trigger is low self-esteem, and food is used as a means of assuaging the pain of difficult emotions around self-worth. Food becomes a substitute for unmet needs such as respect, happiness or fulfilment. While bingeing, the rest of the world vanishes and all that exists is the comfort of eating.

Sufferers will often have problems with depression, anxiety, boredom, anger, sadness and loneliness. Food becomes their only reliable 'friend', a 'safe' way of temporarily relieving unhappiness and numbing the pain. In binge eating disorder, food is used to cope with stress and negative emotions, and the sufferer will feel totally out of control while eating and powerless to stop. People with this disorder will eat regardless of whether they are hungry or full. In short, they just cannot resist food: it is a compulsion over which they have very little control.

 IF YOU REMEMBER ONE THING Binge eating disorder is not based on greed; it is a compulsion that is incredibly difficult to overcome. Sufferers tarred with the label 'greedy' often suffer even lower self-esteem because of it, which intensifies the issue.

Binge eating disorder is very similar to bulimia in terms of bingeing; however, the key difference is that there are no subsequent inappropriate compensatory behaviours. A BED sufferer will not attempt to purge and get rid of the excess calories, nor will they exercise furiously to try to burn the calories off.

Because of this, while sufferers of bulimia tend to be of average or slightly above average weight, individuals with BED can range from normal weight to extreme obesity. A sufferer of BED will, however, carry out many of the practices mentioned in the previous chapter, such as hoarding food for binges and hiding wrappers and containers after bingeing.

In all other regards the sufferer of BED experiences the same feelings of overwhelming disgust, helplessness and depression which a sufferer of bulimia would experience after having binged. They are caught up in a similar cycle, although the BED sufferer, if anything, may feel even greater levels of self-loathing due to what they perceive as the unattractiveness of their overweight body.

This shame and embarrassment makes them even more likely to turn to food as a temporary coping mechanism, to provide relief from these deeply painful negative feelings. Many sufferers of BED not only binge but also graze continuously on food as long as it is present, despite feeling acute discomfort due to being overly full. It is not dissimilar to some people who feel uncomfortable without a cigarette and as a consequence chain-smoke.

BED sufferers frequently 'chain-eat' as a response to their insatiable cravings and intersperse this behaviour with binges. Just as a chain-smoker cannot stop at one cigarette, the sufferer of BED is incapable of resisting the entire box of chocolates or packet of biscuits once they have tasted one. They feel compelled to continue eating until there is literally nothing left, and even then they are already plotting their next binge.

The sufferer's life literally revolves around food from the moment that they awake in the morning until they eventually fall asleep at night. Even before going to sleep there will probably be a final visit to the fridge before getting into bed. Once in bed sleep may prove elusive if there is any food still available in the kitchen, as sufferers will often become fixated on it.

The unstoppable craving will only be silenced once the sufferer has sneaked out of bed, crept downstairs and eaten the food, even if it is in the middle of the night. As you can imagine, this not only causes acute embarrassment but is also very disruptive to their sleep patterns. On top of all of that, going to bed on a heavy stomach is not the most conducive means to acquiring a good night's sleep.

Binge eating disorder is on the increase

Though it is given much less attention, BED is the most common of all the eating disorders and has far more sufferers than anorexia and bulimia combined. BED has only recently been acknowledged as a category or condition in its own right in the *DSM-5*, yet in the UK and the USA, the number of sufferers of this eating disorder is quite alarming.

BED is becoming increasingly prevalent, and one only has to look at any gathering of people today and compare it to 40 years ago to see the visible evidence of this phenomenon. Today we have overweight children and overweight adults in quantities that were unheard of in the not-too-distant past.

The National Centre for Eating Disorders claims that 12 million people in the UK suffer from compulsive overeating to varying degrees. This eating disorder affects both males and females to a very similar extent, with only a slightly higher incidence of females. However, due to the added societal pressure placed on women with regard to the importance of physical attractiveness, they tend to present for treatment more readily than men. This factor might well skew the statistics.

It is a disorder that crosses all echelons of society. No

race, socio-economic class or age group is immune to it, although it is more typical in older adults than in younger demographics.

---

1. Do you feel that you have little willpower over how much you eat and consume far more than what you think is a normal amount?

2. Do you eat large quantities of food very rapidly?

3. Do you eat when you are not physically hungry?

4. Do you eat so much that you feel physically uncomfortable?

5. Are you embarrassed or ashamed by your eating habits so try to eat alone?

6. Do you experience regret and self-disgust after you have eaten so much?

If you answered yes to these questions, it is possible that you might be suffering from BED and should speak to your doctor for further guidance and help.

What causes BED?

As in all eating disorders, low self-esteem is clearly linked to the development of BED, but there is also evidence that genetics plays a part. Being overweight as a child, having a history of yo-yo dieting or suffering from psychological conditions such as depression and anxiety also increase an individual's risk of developing BED.

In addition, people who have been sexually abused are more susceptible to developing BED than those who have not experienced this type of trauma. Some people may use being overweight as a means of punishing themselves for feeling bad or unworthy. Some people may also feel unlovable, so try to repel others by being overweight.

Nurture and the development of BED

Upbringing can play a significant role in the causation of BED. Development of this disorder is more common in people who have grown up in households where food was used as a means of showing love, affection and approval. Snacks and treats may have been used to comfort, distract or reward them as a young child.

Many of us can look back at our own childhood and remember that when we fell over and hurt ourselves, we might well have been given an ice cream or lollipop to help stem the flow of tears. If this only happens occasionally it is not a problem. However, some children are routinely silenced if they complain that they are bored or upset by having a bag of crisps or sweets thrust into their hands.

Equally, children who have grown up in households where food was restricted or withdrawn as a punishment may also be more susceptible to developing BED. Another possible contributory factor in the development of BED is for children who have grown up in a home where their parents or older siblings have been overly preoccupied with dieting and weight loss.

Damage caused by binge eating disorder

A huge number of serious physical problems follow in the wake of BED, chiefly caused by being overweight. Many sufferers of BED are obese, which means they have a BMI of 30 or above (see chapter 9 for more on the BMI). Medical conditions which are found more frequently in people suffering from BED (and overweight people in general) include:

- Type 2 diabetes
- Heart disease
- Cancer
- Sleep apnoea
- High blood pressure
- Gallbladder disease
- High cholesterol
- Adrenal exhaustion fatigue
- Osteoarthritis

Psychological and social consequences of BED

The psychological, emotional and social toll of this psychiatric disorder also carries a very high price. Sufferers often experience mental confusion, low self-esteem, guilt due to their lack of self-control and a deeply embedded sense of self-loathing. This, not unnaturally, increases their susceptibility to developing depression.

The knock-on effects of the intense negative feelings experienced affects the sufferer's willingness to socialize. The consequent isolation reinforces their sense of loneliness, which is one of the key triggers for comfort eating, and thus the vicious cycle is further reinforced.

 Not all overweight people suffer from BED, even if they binge. It must be stressed that there are some people who are overweight and also binge but are perfectly comfortable with their eating habits and suffer no psychological problems as a result. These people do not suffer from BED, since they do not feel out of control and nor do they experience distress about their eating patterns.

However, although these people may not suffer psychological or social distress as a result of their weight – largeness becoming increasingly the norm rather than the exception – this does not mean that they are immune to physical problems as a consequence of being overweight.

 Whether you think you have BED, or whether you simply have bad eating habits, bringing your bingeing under control takes time and effort. Use the charter below to help you think more about your food and to try to avoid binges.

The binge-eater's charter

1. Plan in advance what you intend to eat and compile a detailed, balanced list of food items before shopping.

2. Do not keep in the house any type of food that you know you will be tempted to snack on. If you do want to snack, have some prepared carrots or other healthy options available in the fridge.

3. Never shop while feeling hungry, since this will increase the likelihood of making unwise purchases.

4. Try to shop little and often and preferably accompanied by a supporter who will help you to avoid falling prey to binge purchasing. If this is not possible then shop online to avoid spontaneous purchases that you will later regret.

5. Buy small quantities rather than buying in bulk, even though this may prove to be a little more expensive.

6. Never eat in front of the television or while doing any other activity. Always give your full attention to what you are eating. The only exception to this rule is when you are conversing in company who either know that you are trying to eat moderately or those who do not know that you have a problem. The presence of the latter will act as a brake on the possibility of you bingeing anyway, since you would not want to appear greedy or out of control.

7. Use smaller plates, as this helps to automatically reduce portion sizes. Your smaller plate will look full, which is psychologically more pleasing than the same amount of food on a larger plate.

8. Whenever possible, prepare the food yourself, ensuring that you have enough time for this task. By investing time and effort into careful preparation of your meal you will be less likely to eat it quickly and more inclined to relish it by eating slowly.

9. When preparing food, try to resist the urge to make enough for the next meal. This may appear to be expedient but will only provide an unnecessary temptation for you to eat more than you had originally planned. Remember that the extra effort in cooking twice is far less upsetting than the painful emotions elicited from succumbing to bingeing.

10. Put down your cutlery between each mouthful for at least twelve seconds, as this will slow down your speed of eating. There is a lag between swallowing food and your body registering how full it is, so give your body a chance to catch up.

11. Before consuming each mouthful focus upon how your food looks and smells. This will enable you to take your time over the meal as well as to appreciate what you are eating. Smell has a big impact on how you actually taste your food.

12. Try to concentrate on the flavour, texture and temperature of the food, and try to chew for at least eight seconds before swallowing. (I know that this can be a bit tricky with some foods like ice-cream, but I am sure that you get my drift.) This not only helps you to eat in a slower, more measured manner but also enables you to savour and enjoy your meal.

13. Always try to eat bite-sized amounts rather than putting huge quantities of food onto your fork or spoon.

14. Drink plenty of water before and throughout your meal: approximately 750ml is a good amount to aim for. This will not only help you to feel fuller and reduce your temptation to overeat but also aids digestion.

15. Recognize your established 'activity and food' associations – such as cinema = popcorn; seaside = fish and chips; football = pizza; shopping outing = tea and cake – and decide beforehand what you want to eat instead.

16. Never label any food as 'forbidden', since this only serves to set up cravings in the brain. Instead, allow yourself treats but decide when and how much you intend to consume. If your general food intake consists of sufficient healthy fats, lean proteins, carbohydrates, fruit and vegetables, you can allow yourself the odd indulgence of a not-so-healthy option.

17. NEVER EVER go on an unsustainable diet, since this will only make your body alter its metabolic rate and increase your chances of putting on more weight once the diet has ended. Furthermore, many diets are downright harmful. For example, those that advocate a high intake of proteins at the expense of much else can cause a loss of bone density, and those that ban carbohydrates can reduce your serotonin level and cause low moods. Decide on a healthy and sustainable way of eating and work towards achieving that goal. This will only be found in a balanced diet that includes all food groups.

18. Remember that you are human and therefore not perfect. It is natural to relapse from time to time, and this is more than okay. In fact, it's totally normal. You are so much more than what you eat, so pick yourself up after a relapse and persist with trying to achieve your goals. This is something that you can justifiably be proud of, since it shows true character to carry on in the face of adversity.

19. Always remember that bingeing is a substitute for something that is lacking in your life. Look at yourself holistically and recognize your strengths and qualities. Use this information to discover what really makes you feel alive and fulfilled. I can guarantee that worthwhile relationships, hobbies that you feel passionately about and accepting personal challenges are far more

sustaining than packets of custard creams or a shed-load of iced buns.

20. Reconnect with your body so that you can identify hunger signals and satiety signals. Always be conscious about why you are eating. Are you responding to a physical cue or an emotional cue? By practising mindfulness you will automatically increase your awareness, which will enable you to eat intuitively.

One should eat to live, not live to eat.
Moliere

II. DIAGNOSIS AND SYMPTOMS OF BINGE EATING DISORDER (BED)

Diagnosis, types and symptoms

Diagnosis of binge eating disorder
According to the *DSM-5*, a diagnosis of binge eating disorder is given *only* if all five of the criteria below are met:

1. Repeated episodes of compulsively eating (bingeing) within a short space of time (less than two hours) a quantity of food which is considered vastly excessive when compared with what most people would consume under similar circumstances. The individual experiences feeling out of control while eating the food and may feel that they cannot stop or limit the amount they are eating.

2. The episodes of bingeing as described above are associated with at least three of the following:
   - Eating until feeling uncomfortably full
   - Eating large amounts of food when not feeling physically hungry
   - Eating much more rapidly than normal
   - Eating alone due to embarrassment over the quantity of food consumed
   - Feelings of self-disgust and depression, or feeling intense guilt afterwards.

3. Experiences considerable distress about bingeing

4. Bingeing occurs, on average, at least once a week for three months

5. There is no repeated use of inappropriate compensatory behaviours. The bingeing does not occur exclusively during the course of anorexia, bulimia or avoidant/restrictive food intake disorder (ARFID).

Below are some of the warning signs and symptoms of binge eating disorder.

Psychological signs:
- Preoccupation with food
- Anxiety
- Depression
- Low self-esteem

- Embarrassment about appearance and feeling unattractive
- Acute distress when bingeing and feelings of shame afterwards
- Isolation and loneliness
- Guilt, loathing and self-disgust
- Fearful about disapproval from others
- Feeling out of control when eating and powerless to stop
- Suicidal ideation
- Seldom feeling satisfied
- Sugar cravings
- Feeling driven to consume food incessantly

Physical signs:
- Sleep apnoea
- Headaches
- Skin problems like acne and fungal infections
- High blood pressure
- Kidney problems
- Weight gain
- Sweating
- Tremors

- Chronic back pain

- Asthma

- Stroke

- Irregular menstrual cycle

- Complications during pregnancy

- Muscle and joint pain

- Osteoarthritis

- Heart disease

- Gallbladder disease

- Type 2 diabetes

- High cholesterol

- Gastrointestinal problems

- Mobility problems

- Visual impairment

- Hypertension

Behavioural signs:
- Eating more rapidly than normal

- Eating excessively until uncomfortably full

- Eating normal quantities in public and then gorging privately

- Eating when not hungry

- Eating secretly

- Bingeing frequently, unable to control the compulsion

- Avoiding social gatherings, especially those in which food is involved

- Purchasing vast quantities of food

- Manipulating situations so as to be able to eat alone

- Stockpiling and hiding food

- Indiscriminate eating of food, sometimes still frozen or uncooked

- Eating more at times of stress

- Eating continuously rather than just at mealtimes

- Eating during the night

- Hiding wrappers and food containers

- Stashing food in the car, office desk, garage or shed

Binge eating disorder

Ruby had experienced a difficult relationship with food since childhood, having an intense dislike of vegetables and most fruits. Her parents' marriage had always been very volatile, and verbal and physical abuse was fairly routine. Ruby and her siblings lived in dread of mealtimes, when they would all sit down together as a family and an argument between her parents would inevitably ensue.

The children did their best to stay out of the firing line by rapidly eating their food and then swiftly leaving the table once the meal was over. Ruby, the youngest, would go straight to her bedroom while her brothers would go off to visit friends in the neighbourhood and stay out until almost bedtime.

Due to the parental discord, the children were largely neglected. It went virtually unnoticed that Ruby was picky about her food, along with how distressed she was by the endless shouting and fighting which took place in the family home. Ruby developed an insatiable craving for sugary, fattening foods and found that they helped to shut out her negative emotions.

Once in the safety of her bedroom, Ruby would comfort eat by consuming entire malt loaves along with bars of chocolate and bags of sweets. This served to give her temporary relief and drown out the noise of her parents rowing downstairs. Her maternal grandmother also tried to compensate for the hostile environment in which her grandchildren lived by supplying them with these food treats, which meant that Ruby further associated food with feeling better emotionally.

Ruby would agree to do chores for her brothers in exchange for their supply of treats and as a consequence rapidly became very overweight. At school, she was cruelly teased by the other children about her size and they nicknamed her Nelly, after the eponymous elephant of the popular children's song.

Apart from her well-intentioned but misguided grand-mother, Ruby had nobody in whom she could confide about her deep unhappiness and insecurity. As the fighting continued at home and the comfort eating escalated, Ruby's weight steadily increased. Ruby hated the ridicule that she encountered but tried to laugh it off by saying she didn't care. She would sometimes show off that she could eat four doughnuts before anyone else could finish one.

Although laughing and jolly on the outside, deep down Ruby hated herself. She felt fat, ugly, useless and worth-less. In short, Ruby despised herself and even erroneously blamed herself for her parents' unhappy marriage. As far as Ruby was concerned, she was totally bad and her only sanctuary from these painful emotions was bingeing.

Having binged she invariably felt nauseous and disgusted by her greed. The tightness and consequent discomfort of her school uniform served as a constant reminder of her out-of-control behaviour, and Ruby felt her shame acutely. She would stuff all the empty packaging from her bingeing session into her school bag and dispose of the evidence on her way to school.

After leaving school, Ruby acquired a job in a super-market, working on the checkout. Because of her cheerful banter and friendly, helpful disposition, the customers universally liked her. However, her colleagues shunned her and made nasty, caustic comments about her size.

Despite taking normal portions of food from the super-market canteen she was still mocked by the staff, who would often teasingly ask if she would like a double helping. The cashier made one particularly cutting remark when she went to pay for her modest meal. He looked at her tray and loudly announced: 'That's like feeding an elephant a grape.' The 'elephant' comment immediately acted as an unpleasant reminder of all of the teasing she had endured at school.

The sedentary nature of her employment and being constantly surrounded by food made Ruby's weight problem even more acute. During lulls in the working day she would mentally plan for the next binge. On finishing work, she would drive to a shopping centre and visit three or four shops where she would purchase huge quantities of food. She would alternate which shops she visited each evening to lessen the attention that her purchases seemed to arouse in the sales staff.

Once back at home Ruby would leave her stash of food in the car and check to see if the coast was clear. Once assured that nobody was around she would unload her car and carry her shopping upstairs to her bedroom where she would hide it in the wardrobe. Once the evening meal was over, Ruby would pretend that she had to calls to make and would retire to her room, lock the door and secretly binge. This solitary behaviour went on for years and Ruby, apart from going to work and purchasing food, became a prisoner in her room with no friends or social life.

By the age of 26, Ruby suffered from severe backache, headaches and sleep apnoea. Walking short distances made her feel totally breathless. By the time that she had completed her shift at the checkout Ruby was utterly exhausted and could scarcely drag herself to the car park. Recognizing that her excess weight was making her physically ill, Ruby had unsuccessfully tried diet pills and Weight Watchers but could not give up the bingeing.

The more Ruby failed to resist bingeing, the more she hated herself for her perceived weakness and greed. Eventually Ruby's self-loathing became so acute that she attempted to take her own life by taking an overdose of pills. Luckily her brother discovered her in time and called an ambulance. After Ruby's release from hospital her GP prescribed a course of anti-depressants and outpatient treatment.

Ruby is slowly managing to eat a more healthy range of foods, including vegetables and fruits. She has moved out of the family home and feels far less agitated away from the conflict caused by her parents' constant arguing. Ruby swims regularly and has recourse to a helpline when she feels the urge to binge. Most importantly, Ruby has made some friends from the self-help group, which she attends on a weekly basis.

By sharing experiences within the group, she now feels less isolated and less of a failure. The group has acted as a catalyst towards recovery. Ruby, encouraged by the others in the group, has taken up the practice of mindfulness. This has taught her to be more self-aware and less reactive to the triggers that lead to her bingeing. She has learnt to be kinder towards herself and is beginning to recognize her strengths instead of purely focusing upon her weaknesses.

Her progress has been further augmented by weekly sessions with a counsellor with whom Ruby has built a trusting relationship. Within counselling, she has started to address the very deep painful emotions that underpin her eating disorder. Although there have been many setbacks along the way and there is still some distance to go, Ruby feels optimistic and hopeful that as the frequency of bingeing is reduced she will lose her excess weight along with her self-hatred and will eventually make a full recovery.

8. Pica disorder

The chains of habit are too weak to be felt
until they are too strong to be broken.
Samuel Johnson

I. UNDERSTANDING PICA DISORDER

The term 'pica' is derived from the Latin word for magpie, possibly due to the bird's distinct lack of discernment with regard to what it eats. The range of non-nutritive substances which may be consumed by pica disorder sufferers is very diverse, and some substances have their own distinct medical categories. For example:

- Amylophagia: consumption of starch

- Geophagia: consumption of soil substances, e.g. clay, chalk, mud

- Papophagia: consumption of ice

- Coprophagia: consumption of faeces

- Xylophagia: consumption of wood, e.g. pencils, paper

- Urophagia: consumption of urine

- Trichophagia: consumption of hair or wool

- Hylophagia: consumption of glass, e.g. light bulbs

- Lithophagia: consumption of pebbles, stones and rocks

- Mucophagia: consumption of mucus

Other substances which have been documented as being consumed by pica disorder sufferers include paint, jewellery, plaster, coins, cigarette butts, toothpaste, rubber, drawing pins, sand, charcoal, nails, string, screws, leaves, needles, soap, sponges, magnets, glue, insects, bones, buttons, talcum powder, pens and laundry detergent.

Cigarette butts deserve a special mention since they contain some very dangerous chemicals. As a response to this danger a group has been formed called the Pica Task Force in an attempt to raise public awareness that people with development disabilities are attracted to this hazardous waste. They urge the public to dispose of cigarette butts with care and consideration to help protect this vulnerable sector of the population.

Who is susceptible to pica disorder?

Pica disorder tends to afflict mainly children and adults with intellectual disabilities, but it can also affect pregnant women who experience cravings, as well as people with none of these conditions. Evidence from recent surveys show that the proportion of pregnant women who experience cravings of both the harmful and harmless variety is steadily rising compared to previous generations.

Pregnant women and cravings

 Ask your female friends, relatives and colleagues who have children whether they had cravings while pregnant. Do you find the incidence of cravings more prolific in the younger generations?

It should be stressed that most pregnant women develop cravings for food substances such as chocolate, spices, pickles, salt, dairy products, citrus fruits, cakes and/or sweets. These cravings are deemed to be harmless, providing that the woman does not neglect to adhere to a balanced, nutritious diet. Also, some pregnant women satisfy their cravings by smell alone, for example by sniffing leather, shoe polish, detergents, bleach, tyres or tar. However, there are a number of women who actually consume non-nutritive substances, which can cause considerable damage to their health and qualify them for a diagnosis of pica disorder.

According to a recent survey, the ingestion of ice is the most popular craving in pregnant women. This seemingly harmless craving can cause dental problems, jaw strain and inhibit peristalsis in the digestive system. According to the report, the other common non-nutritive cravings, in order of popularity, are: coal, toothpaste, sponges, mud, chalk, soap, matches and rubber. As you will appreciate, these substances can cause serious harm, and women experiencing these cravings should consult their doctor.

 Unfortunately, pica disorder often remains undiagnosed, particularly in pregnant women. Despite recognizing that their behaviour is both unhealthy and outside of their normal eating patterns, many pregnant women are reluctant to seek medical help. This is due to the strong compulsion to ingest these non-nutritive substances, which makes it hard to want to stop, as well as due to their embarrassment and shame at the thought of disclosing this behaviour to their doctor. But pica is a real disorder, and if you (or someone you know) suspect you have it, it's important to seek help to make sure you don't do yourself harm.

What causes pica disorder?

Many theories abound as to what causes pica, ranging from stress to nutritional deficiencies, parental neglect or abuse, to name but a few. But there is little hard evidence to support these theories, and the causes of pica disorder remain largely a mystery. However, it is generally accepted that the disorder stems mainly from psychological causes, as even when mineral deficiencies exist, the substances consumed do not redress the deficiency. Pica disorder has also been convincingly linked with obsessive-compulsive disorder (OCD).

Dangers of pica disorder

There are many serious dangers resulting from pica disorder, depending on the substances consumed. These include, but are not limited to, worm infestations and parasitic infection from soil and faeces, lead poisoning from plaster and paint, and gastrointestinal problems such as bowel perforation, blocked or torn intestines and ulcers from the ingestion of glass or sharp metals. Lead toxicity is considered the most common consequence of pica disorder and can cause serious mental impairment, as well as death in severe cases.

II. DIAGNOSIS AND SYMPTOMS OF PICA DISORDER

According to the *DSM-5*, the following criteria must be met to warrant a diagnosis of pica disorder:

1. The repeated consumption of non-nutritive substances for at least one month.

2. The eating of these substances is inappropriate for the developmental stage of the individual, which means that the sufferer is usually over two years old (since babies from six months old to approximately two years old naturally explore by putting things into their mouths).

3. The behaviour is not considered to be a cultural or religious norm and therefore is not socially acceptable.

Where it is recognized as a traditional practice, it is viewed as adaptive behaviour and would not qualify for pica disorder diagnosis. An example of this is clay ingestion in parts of Africa.

4. It must be sufficiently severe to require medical attention in its own right, if it arises concurrently with another medical disorder such as autism, or as the result of another condition such as pregnancy.

Symptoms and signs of pica

Obviously, the clearest sign of pica is the craving and ingestion of non-food substances. But as these substances are often consumed in secret, the disorder can be difficult to detect. Sadly, therefore, it is often the physical symptoms of poisoning, infections, ruptures and tears to the gut that provide the first indication that someone is suffering from pica disorder.

Treatment of pica

The treatment offered will depend on the type of pica disorder that has been diagnosed. If there are physical concerns with regard to the person's health then these will be remedied first by giving the patient supplements to make up for any mineral deficiencies. Sometimes hospitalization is essential and the patient will undergo surgery to repair the damage caused by the objects ingested.

Once the person's physical health has been stabilized, psychological treatment will then be offered. In some cases this will take the form of individual or family counselling. In cases where the sufferer experiences intellectual impairment, behavioural therapy has proved useful to help the individual to break their compulsive habit. Support groups, cognitive behavioural therapy, nutritional education, individual counselling and the use of drugs such as selective serotonin reuptake inhibitors (SSRIs) have proved beneficial in helping sufferers to overcome this disorder.

CASE STUDY

Pica
Sub-type: Xylophagia
Ferdinand had grown up in a very busy household where little time was dedicated to the children and everyone was expected to manage their own problems. From a young age, Ferdinand had fallen into the habit of chewing the end of his pencil. This seemed to give him some comfort and helped him to relax.

As he progressed through school this habit escalated, and he would take the pencil shavings home from the sharpener on the teacher's desk on the pretext of emptying it for her, but in reality so that he could eat them. Ferdinand's habit continued to get worse and he started to eat entire pencils as well as paper tissues. By the age of 21, the cravings had become so bad that he was consuming half a box of tissues and three pencils per day. It was not until he was in a relationship with his girlfriend Mia that he was prepared to admit to himself how out of control he felt about this strange addiction.

Together they sought help and after visiting his GP, Ferdinand was given medication and referred to a cognitive behavioural therapist. As a result of this treatment he has managed to slow down his consumption of wood-based matter and continues to reduce his pencil and tissue intake on a weekly basis.

Having discussed the diagnosis and symptoms of the various types of problematic eating, it is essential once a problem has been identified to seek help and support; so, in the next section of the book we will look at various treatments that might come into play once someone is diagnosed with an eating disorder.

PART TWO
Treating Problem Eating

9. A note on
the body mass index (BMI)

In this second section of the book we will look at the various treatments available for problem eating, and how you access them. But before we do, I'd like to first look at one of the most commonly used (and abused) tools for measuring weight: the BMI. The term 'body mass index', commonly referred to as BMI, is often bandied about when discussing people who have an eating disorder. BMI is a way of calculating an individual's body shape based on the person's height and weight, as follows:

BMI = a person's body mass (weight), divided by the square of their height

$$BMI = \frac{mass\ (kilograms)}{(height\ (metres))^2}$$

Although it is extremely widely used, BMI is a rather rough and ready tool for showing how much an individual's body weight deviates from what is believed to be 'normal' or average for someone of that height. For one thing, it does not differentiate between body fat and muscle, the latter being far heavier than the former. For this reason, serious athletes often come out with a BMI that classes them as overweight, even though this is evidently not the case.

There are also many other anomalies that prevent this diagnostic tool being a totally accurate instrument. For example, it is less reliable when used on people with bulimic features, fluid restriction or other physical comorbidities. It is also quite easy to trick: many sufferers of anorexia drink vast quantities of water before being weighed to prevent an accurate BMI reading. It has also been proven to be less reliable in very tall people.

The biggest problem with the BMI is that this imprecise tool appears to have become the gold standard for indicating whether someone is entitled to treatment or not. As mentioned earlier, patients with serious problems are often sent away by their GP because their BMI is not low enough! The BMI ranges – which determine what constitutes underweight, normal, overweight and obese – take into account a number of key factors such as age, sex and developmental stage. However, there are other significant factors which are not part of the calculation. In addition, there are international variations when comparing ranges. In Hong Kong, for example, anyone with a BMI of 30 or over is considered severely obese, whereas in the UK a person would have to have a BMI of over 40 to be ascribed to this category.

The BMI was originally designed for use in comparing weight in different populations and was not intended for individual diagnosis: it is meant for measuring trends, not unique cases. So, while it can be a useful tool, it is not the be-all and end-all of measuring weight.

Below are the current BMI categories in the UK:

BMI range	Category
Less than 15	Very severely underweight
15 to 16	Severely underweight
16 to 18.5	Underweight
18.5 to 25	Normal healthy weight
25 to 30	Overweight
30 to 35	Obese Class 1 (Moderately obese)
35 to 40	Obese Class 2 (Severely obese)
Over 40	Obese Class 3 (Very severely obese)

Find an online BMI calculator and calculate your BMI. Where do you fall on the scale? Are there any mitigating factors that could affect your result?

Luckily, many doctors now use other tests to determine eligibility for treatment, including:

- Blood tests

- Examination of muscle strength

- Measuring pulse rate (lying and standing)

- Peripheral circulation tests

- Measuring core temperature

- Measuring blood pressure (lying and standing)

- Examining the skin for dryness

- Examining the patient physically for nutritional deficiencies or infection.

 Testing muscle strength is very easy to do if you are concerned about someone with an eating disorder (or you can try them yourself). Here are two simple tests you can try.

Test 1: The sit-up test
Ask the person to lie flat on their back on the floor and then do a sit-up without using their hands.

Test 2: The squat test
Ask the person to squat on their haunches and then stand up without using their arms.

---

10. Treatments

*The secret of happiness is freedom, and
the secret of freedom, courage.*
Thucydides

Before exploring treatment options for problematic eating, I would like to re-emphasize that eating disorders can be fierce opponents. A great deal of courage is required to ensure that they are defeated. The following key points should be borne in mind:

1. The problem must be identified and acknowledged by the sufferer. It is not possible to help someone who refuses to see that they have a problem in the first place. Ultimately, help and treatments can only work with the sufferer's co-operation. The sufferer needs to be ready to seek help and want to make the necessary changes to achieve the goal of recovery.

2. It is often necessary to triangulate treatment approaches and to keep searching and implementing different therapies until success is achieved. Eating disorders are very complex psychiatric illnesses and each sufferer's experience is unique. There is little point in treating the symptoms without discovering the underlying causes. For this reason, a holistic approach attending to the

mind, body and spirit is usually the most successful means of establishing an enduring recovery.

3. Patience, determination, courage, commitment and time are all essential ingredients in overcoming an eating disorder. These qualities are not just required by the sufferers but also by those who are accompanying them on their journey back to health. It is no secret within the psychiatric community that working with patients with eating disorders takes the highest toll on the welfare of the nurses and practitioners who support them. For this reason, intense levels of peer support and professional supervision are essential to maintain morale and keep hope alive, and the same is needed for carers of eating disorder sufferers.

Treatment approaches

As well as the use of different types of therapy, the level of care can vary in intensity as follows:

- Intensive hospitalization with an eating disorder programme

- Partial hospitalization

- Intensive outpatient treatment with an eating disorder programme

- Weekly eating disorder therapy groups

- Individual therapy (various approaches)

- Self-help groups for sufferers and/or carers

- Family education and self-help books

Which treatment is appropriate will depend on the severity of the condition but also on factors such as:

1. The disposition of the client

2. The type of problem eating

3. The duration of the problem

4. The sufferer's physical condition or degree of wellness

5. The sufferer's level of motivation for change.

Sometimes waiting lists can be very over-subscribed for the few treatment resources offered by the state, and individuals may seek out private healthcare options. A further complication with regard to recovery from eating disorders is that in some stubborn cases, treatment needs to be long-term, and medical insurance policies may not provide the necessary coverage. These added financial strains can further compound the burden for families who are trying to support a sufferer of an eating disorder.

 Before embarking on a discussion of the various forms of available treatments, I would like to reiterate the importance of first establishing the medical stability of the sufferer. There is no point in offering psychological therapy to someone who is in imminent danger of heart or kidney failure.

A severely malnourished client must first have their physical nutritional needs sufficiently secured before attempting to address the underlying causes of their eating distress. Once a safe level of physical stability is achieved, medical and psychological treatments can then work concurrently.

The GP is often the first port of call when a person is ready to acknowledge they have an eating disorder. Hopefully, the GP will be able to advise you of what is available in your area in terms of treatment and support. Some areas have inpatient and outpatient specialist eating disorder units available, but others only offer non-specialist hospital admission. There may be self-help groups available or counselling within the GP's practice; every area has different resources. Others will first visit a private therapist or psychiatrist, who should also be able to point them in the direction of the help available in their area.

 It is extremely important before undertaking any form of private treatment that you check out the training and qualifications of your intended practitioner. Bona fide therapists will usually be registered with a governing body. Sadly, there are still a number of cowboys out there who can do more harm than good, so please exercise due diligence to ensure that your

practitioner has regular supervision and ongoing professional development.

In the following chapters I would like to offer a brief synopsis
of several different approaches used in treating people who
suffer from eating disorders. As I have articulated earlier in
the book, each sufferer responds to treatments differently.
There is no such thing as a one-size-fits-all approach that
will suit everyone.

For this reason, I intend to cover a wide range of therapies, from mainstream approaches to complementary
treatments. Complementary treatments are used as an
adjunct to other approaches, rather than as a stand-alone
approach. Having said this, even mainstream treatments are
often used in conjunction with other modalities. All of this
indicates that our current state of knowledge for treating
eating disorders still has a long way to go before we know
the most efficacious way of curing these potentially lethal
illnesses.

One form of treatment that has achieved impressive
empirical results is the Maudsley approach (see chapter 14),
and for this reason I will go into greater depth in describing
this treatment.

11. Mainstream therapies and treatments

*The greatest revolution of our generation
is the discovery that human beings, by
changing the inner attitudes of their minds,
can change the outer aspect of their lives.*
William James

Cognitive analytic therapy (CAT)

CAT has many similarities with cognitive behavioural therapy (CBT, explored in detail in pp. 152–6) in that they are both highly focused, brief therapies that use a collaborative approach. CAT uses a more interpersonal methodology in that the client and practitioner will identify issues together, and more importance is placed on the interactions within the therapeutic relationship.

CAT encourages the client to take up the observer stance in their own life, instead of being helplessly embroiled in their behaviour, incapable of seeing the wood for the trees. They are encouraged to observe, experience, recognize and name the patterns of thought, feelings and behaviour that they live with and to share this with the practitioner.

As a consequence of this shared understanding, the client can dispassionately see what is working and what is not and thus change their ensconced behaviours and attitudes and make more constructive choices.

Approximately twenty hourly sessions are needed for CAT, with several follow-up sessions once the therapy has been completed. These sessions can be highly creative, involving journals, self-reflection, writing and movement. These sessions consist of several phases, namely:

- **The formulation phase:** Information is gathered about the client's life experience and personal history, including successes and failures.

- **The reformulation letter phase:** A written synopsis is created of the shared understanding of the issues explored in therapy. This also looks at the changes undertaken by the client and how they are coping. This active stage involves the client and practitioner working together, mapping out and identifying patterns of relating, feeling and acting. By monitoring together what works and what maintains destructive patterns, they are then in a position to know how to revise these patterns into formats that are constructive.

- **The ending phase:** Terminating this intense collaborative exercise can be daunting, so the final sessions are dedicated to acknowledging that the work has come to an end. Both parties will write a 'goodbye letter' to mark the completion of their therapeutic relationship.

I find that this refreshingly contemporary form of therapy can be highly effective for sufferers of eating disorders:

instead of becoming mired in the past, it enables a client to focus on the here and now.

An individual can work with the practitioner to change their state of mind in the present moment. This is largely encouraged by the example set by the therapist to be upfront and honest. This high degree of openness and collaboration is an intrinsic factor in the success of this form of treatment.

The National Institute for Health and Care Excellence (NICE) guidelines endorse CAT for sufferers of anorexia in particular; however, there is clear evidence that it also helps sufferers of bulimia.

Cognitive behavioural therapy (CBT)

Cognitive behavioural therapy explores the unhealthy thoughts and emotions underlying an eating disorder. It works upon the premise that how we think influences how we feel, which ultimately affects how we behave. CBT is one of the most successful treatments for anorexia and bulimia, as well as for other eating disorders and mental health problems. It is often used in conjunction with relaxation techniques and enables the sufferer to explore their behaviour on a day-to-day basis.

The therapist will help the client to identify what are known as cognitive distortions, or thinking errors, which lead to irrational thoughts. There are a wide variety of distortions, such as personalizing information or black-and-white thinking. A typical example of this all-or-nothing approach would be a client starting each day by thinking: 'Today I must eat like a normal person and will not binge or purge, otherwise I will be a failure.'

The therapist would help them to rethink this statement to make it more rational rather than setting themself up for failure. It might be changed to: 'Today I will try my best to eat like a normal person, but if I lapse in any way I will forgive myself and remain focused on recovery.'

Sufferers are encouraged to keep a journal or food diary to enable them to examine the triggers of their destructive eating behaviours. These are known as 'activating events'. Examples of activating events could range from stress caused by having to work overtime to disappointment due to a cancelled arrangement to anger over a friend's disloyalty.

The sufferer then explores their beliefs around the activating event that has triggered their negative eating pattern. For example, it could be a fundamental belief that people take advantage of them and expect them to work overtime because they are unworthy. Or they will reason that because they don't matter, people don't care about cancelling arrangements at short notice. Or they might think that their lack of worthiness means that others will not consider their feelings and will be disloyal.

These warped and erroneous beliefs bring in their wake some very daunting emotions, which in turn generate destructive behaviours as the sufferer tries to avoid or suppress their feelings. These behaviours could be self-punishment exercises like starvation, excessive exercising or self-harming, or compensatory behaviours to make up for their hurt feelings, such as comfort eating and bingeing.

With the support of the therapist, the sufferer is encouraged to challenge their dysfunctional thought processes by providing evidence to support their views. Having disputed their false premises, they can then experiment with implementing healthier, more realistic beliefs.

As a consequence of more constructive beliefs, they will generate more positive and empowering feelings. The sufferer will then be able to break the vicious cycle of self-destructive behaviour and start to tap into a more virtuous cycle, since they no longer experience the compulsion to suppress painful emotions.

A food diary is an excellent method for helping the sufferer to trace patterns of behaviour back to particular triggers, as it encourages them to stop to think about why they behaved in a certain way. In addition, as they become more thoughtful and self-aware, the food diary acts as an incentive, since they can visibly see that they have reduced bingeing, purging, laxative use or self-starvation over several weeks.

If you are suffering from problem eating, use a form like the one below to monitor your eating behaviour. Photocopy the blank form on page 156 and use it as a food diary over the next two weeks to see if you can identify patterns of events that trigger thoughts, emotions and behaviour that affect your food intake. By reflecting on your state of mind when these triggers/activating events occur, you will be able to develop a high degree of self-awareness. This will enable you to intercept the negative thoughts and challenge them. You will then be able to implement new strategies to induce more constructive behaviours.

A sample entry might look as follows ('B' stands for binged and 'V' stands for vomited):

Date/ time	Food consumed	B	V	L	D	E	Causes and consequences
7.00pm	Whole tub of ice cream; Box of cereal with cream	Y	Y				Lost some important work on my computer by not saving it properly. Felt really frustrated. It confirmed I was a loser and totally incapable of doing anything right. Went to the kitchen and started to binge. Felt disgusted by my lack of self-control – hate myself. Felt I had to get rid of the calories so made myself vomit.

Food journal

B = Binge; V = Vomited; L = Laxatives; D = Diuretics; E = Excessive exercise

Date/time	Food consumed	B	V	L	D	E	Causes and consequences

Counselling and psychotherapy

Counselling and psychotherapy are umbrella terms that cover a range of talking therapies. They are delivered by trained practitioners who work with people over a short or long term to help them bring about effective change or enhance their well-being.
British Association for Counselling and Psychotherapy

Counselling and psychotherapy are generic terms that are used interchangeably since there is no consensus within the profession as to what differentiates one from the other. For the sake of simplicity, I shall only use the term 'counselling', but this refers to psychotherapy too.

As you can see from the above BACP definition, counselling is a form of talking therapy. Regardless of the particular type of counselling, of which there are hundreds, the key factor that they all have in common is the importance of the quality of the therapeutic relationship. Counsellors are trained in specific approaches and some use just one approach, for example, psychoanalysis, while others use a combination, which is known as an eclectic or integrative approach.

Counselling provides an opportunity for an individual to explore deeply private aspects of their life in a safe and confidential environment with a trained practitioner. It is imperative that the client feels totally accepted, respected and valued to enable them to trust their counsellor. They must not feel judged in any way, as this would inhibit the client in exploring their true feelings.

It is the counsellor's role to facilitate the client in mobilizing their own resources so that they can deal with their difficulties effectively. A skilled practitioner will be able to empathize with the client's perspective, and being understood in this way enables the client to explore their options in a non-defensive manner.

Some forms of counselling are more directive (i.e. counsellor-led) than others, but all types seek to encourage the client in finding their own solutions. Through communicating and feeling that their thoughts are being heard, the client begins to accept themself, validates their own emotions and learns new ways of expressing powerful feelings such as anger, fear or sorrow in constructive ways rather than through the abuse of food intake.

Clients suffering from eating disorders can often feel ashamed about their behaviour and have frequently been judged in a pejorative fashion by others. Within the safety of the therapeutic alliance, the client can address their concerns without needing to worry if they are pleasing or disappointing the counsellor. This can be a unique experience for an individual who has been oppressed by others who pressurize them to be or look a certain way.

The counsellor is present in the capacity of a facilitator rather than as a party with a vested interest in the outcome, which is often the case with family and friends. The nature of this relationship offers the client far greater freedom to express themself and discover their true being, which is very liberating for sufferers of eating disorders.

It is difficult to estimate the number of sessions needed to support a client who is recovering from an eating disorder. Counsellors using the human givens approach tend to work in a short-term manner, whereas those using a person-centred approach may require many more sessions. Other key factors are the nature and personality of the client and the duration of the illness. The less ensconced the negative habits, the easier it is to relearn constructive ones.

Human givens approach

This is a talking therapy that rapidly identifies which of the client's emotional needs are not being met and then targets this deficit by exploring the client's natural resources to enable them to meet these needs. The approach sees all mental health issues as stemming from our basic needs not being met, such as the need for security, control, meaning and purpose. It purports that nature has endowed us with the means of meeting these needs from within ourselves or from our environment and that it is just a case of mobilizing our resources to do so.

Person-centred approach

This approach seeks to provide a particular therapeutic environment by means of six conditions, which will facilitate the client in finding their own answers to their problems. (For more on this, look up the writings of Carl Rogers.) The practitioner is not seen as the expert but rather as a facilitator who enables the client to recognize that he or she is the expert in their own life. It is based upon the premise that we all possess what is called an actualizing tendency, which seeks to find fulfilment of our potential. How long this therapy will take depends upon the client's ability to trust the relationship, but by feeling understood and not judged they will learn to trust themself.

Specialist treatment centres

There are a number of specialist treatment centres available, offering both inpatient and outpatient treatment programmes for eating disorders. Outpatient or day-care treatment is when the patient spends the day at the unit but spends the night at home. These programmes can vary in cost and intensity. The most successful programmes offer a personalized service catering to the individual needs of the sufferer. They offer a combination of one-on-one as well as group sessions, both of which offer different benefits for the client.

The treatment approach is holistic and will address all the components involved in sustainable recovery. The emotional, spiritual, physical, relational and nutritional needs of the sufferer will be explored and treated by highly experienced specialists. In some clinics, medical staff conduct biochemical assessments and can treat chemical dependency issues on-site. Some centres encourage family participation and offer nutritional education.

Interpersonal psychotherapy

Interpersonal psychotherapy is a short-term therapy, usually lasting up to twenty weeks, consisting of the initial, intermediate and termination phases (in a similar way to CAT, see pp. 150–52). These phases are roughly four, twelve and four weeks long respectively.

The initial phase covers assessment, understanding of the problem and goal-setting. The intermediate phase is the action stage when strategies are put into practice to achieve the goals. The final or termination phase consists of reviewing the treatment, evaluating outcomes, planning for future progress and ending the therapeutic relationship.

The treatment targets four key areas: role transitions, interpersonal deficits, grief and interpersonal disputes. It originated as a form of therapy to treat depression but has been modified to treat eating disorders. It is particularly successful for binge eating disorder, but is also used for treating bulimia and anorexia.

By looking at established relationship behaviours and patterns, it facilitates a person who is suffering from an eating disorder to adapt to their current situation or role. By encouraging and teaching new relational skills, the sufferer is able to let go of the destructive behaviour that has helped to maintain the eating disorder.

Medication and medical interventions

Medication is sometimes used alongside other treatment plans. As previously mentioned, it is essential to address the underlying causes of an eating disorder and not just suppress the symptoms. Eating disorders frequently go hand in hand with depression, not least because of the self-loathing and social isolation that these illnesses foster. Some sufferers may be prescribed anti-depressants to sufficiently lift their mood to enable them to access other therapies.

In some cases anti-anxiety medication will prove useful to treat obsessive-compulsive disorder or generalized anxiety, which can often accompany an eating disorder. Many people who have eating disorders, particularly sufferers of anorexia, have great trouble sleeping properly. In such cases their GP might prescribe medication to help to treat insomnia.

In extreme cases of obesity resulting from binge eating disorder, a sufferer may be advised by their medical practitioner to undergo a surgical procedure to fit a gastric band. This is a very serious operation in which the stomach is stapled to reduce its size. The radical reduction in stomach capacity makes it physically impossible for the sufferer to continue to consume enormous amounts of food as previously but does not change the psychological landscape that led the sufferer to overeat in the first place. This procedure is usually only undertaken after all other suitable options have been exhausted and have failed, and when the dangers of obesity outweigh the dangers of surgery.

Sectioning and refeeding

In extreme cases, a sufferer of an eating disorder may need to be sectioned, involving enforced admittance to hospital for treatment. Within the eating disorder community, it is mainly those suffering from anorexia that might require sectioning. Often, in the case of someone suffering from serious malnutrition, the first medical intervention will be to gradually increase and stabilize the patient's dangerously low weight. Refeeding needs expert medical attention to prevent what is called refeeding syndrome: a dangerous medical condition caused by feeding a malnourished body too quickly.

The term **refeeding syndrome** (RS) was coined after the Second World War when prisoners of war who had been starved by the Japanese were released into the care of United States representatives in the Philippines. It was discovered that people who had ingested a negligible amount of food for five days or more were at severe risk of suffering from RS, which is caused by introducing food too rapidly into a previously starved person. RS results in the development of pulmonary, neuromuscular, haematologic, electrolyte and cardiac complications. The most common cause of death by unmonitored refeeding is cardiac arrhythmia. Death can often be preceded by the sufferer experiencing confusion, convulsions or lapsing into a coma.

When can someone be sectioned?

In the UK, if someone is in critical danger of losing their life, for example, due to their refusal to consume food or fluids or because of the risk of self-harming escalating to dangerous levels, then sectioning under the Mental Health Act 1983 may be invoked *under strict parameters*.

It must be stressed that this decision should not be taken lightly and should only be invoked if compelling evidence exists that the sufferer refuses to be hospitalized on a voluntary basis and that no suitable alternative support exists within the community. To take away someone's liberty is very serious indeed and can only be done if compelling evidence exists to support this decision.

To be sectioned, an individual must be suffering from a mental disorder to such an extent that either:

A. The individual's health and safety is at serious risk

or

B. The individual could put other people's lives at risk.

Clearly, it is the first criterion which would be most likely to apply to a person suffering from anorexia; the second criterion might be more applicable to someone suffering from, say, schizophrenia. However, if the individual is in charge of a child, then it could be argued that the second criterion may also be relevant.

How does the sectioning process work?

The stages of sectioning are described below:

1. A mental health assessment (MHA) takes place. This could be triggered by
   a. A mental health team already involved with the individual
   b. A family experiencing serious concerns for a relative's welfare and seeking help
   c. The emergency services.

2. It takes a minimum of three people involved in the MHA to agree that the individual meets the risks described above and that detention is the only possible option. Usually, this consists of at least two doctors and might include an approved mental health professional specifically qualified to conduct a MHA, such as a social worker.

3. Factors involved in the assessment of risk will include:
   a. Medical risk
   b. Psychological risk
   c. Psychosocial risk
   d. Insight/capacity and motivation.

4. Family members can appeal this decision and have the right to apply for discharge of their relative by giving three days' written notice to the hospital managers. This can be blocked by the person in charge of the individual's treatment if they believe that criteria A or B still exist, that is, they would be a danger to themself or to others.

5. Having been sectioned, the individual is entitled to free aftercare once they are discharged.

IF YOU REMEMBER ONE THING

Restricting an individual's liberty can only happen if they are incapable of making an informed choice.

Compulsory treatment can only be justified to prevent self-imposed starvation when an individual literally lacks the capacity to make a rational decision.

As a result of their condition, the sufferer must be incapable of recognizing the consequences of their actions, that is, that starvation will lead to their death. They must either be in denial of their situation or their knowledge must be clouded by their unjustified belief that they are obese.

A refeeding programme must be conducted with considerable attention to detail to prevent serious consequences. In extreme cases, refeeding will be done with the aid of a naso-gastric tube, which feeds nutrients directly into the patient's stomach. Even when administered with great care, the patient will be liable to experience colicky abdominal pain, nausea, reflux symptoms and a strong feeling of fullness, despite having consumed a comparatively small amount of food.

While there are a number of ways in which these gastrointestinal problems can be alleviated by medication, the main message to be taken on board is that refeeding of very malnourished sufferers of anorexia should not be attempted without professional help.

12. Other forms of help

Success is dependent on effort.
Sophocles

Nutritional counselling

Some sufferers of eating disorders have spent many years with their condition and have become totally out of touch with what a normal, balanced diet looks like. For people in this category, nutritional counselling and advice can provide the necessary information and confidence to achieve a healthy diet. The sufferer's previous disordered eating may well have caused nutritional deficiencies that need to be addressed with supplements, and the nutritionist can advise them appropriately.

The nutritional therapist will impart basic nutritional information, such as the recommended intake of minerals, vitamins, liquids and general food requirements for a healthy mind and body. The therapist will also work with the client to design healthy, balanced menus that incorporate all the different food groups.

It is important for the sufferer to learn how to recognize when food is being eaten for emotional reasons rather than to assuage hunger. Sufferers are also taught how to identify their fears surrounding particular foods and learn about the potential consequences to their health of not incorporating these foods in their diet.

Self-help groups

Independent self-help groups can provide a safe place where a sufferer or a carer can express their fears and concerns in a non-judgemental arena. These groups usually include at least two facilitators who ensure that the ground rules are applied to maintain safety and confidentiality. Carers can learn from sufferers and vice versa; this cross-fertilization of information and knowledge can be very reassuring and empowering.

Often, groups offer an excellent library of books concerning eating disorders, which the attendees are invited to borrow. Leaflets and information about where to seek help are also made available. The benefits of knowing that you are not alone with your problem and hearing how others have coped can be very uplifting. The power of being listened to with empathy should never be underestimated. It is often as a result of this positive group experience that people suffering from an eating disorder feel ready to commit to the journey towards recovery.

Twelve-step approach (TSA)

The twelve-step approach is a programme advocated by Eating Disorders Anonymous and models the twelve-step approach of Alcoholics Anonymous. This voluntary fellowship consists of members who suffer from eating disorders and who wish to recover. Meeting up with like-minded people enables mutual support, encouragement and the sharing of good practice to facilitate recovery.

Groups usually meet at least once a week and operate under a system of sponsors or recovery mentors who are appointed to support individuals on their journey towards recovery. This approach does not suit everyone, but for those who are in tune with the underpinning philosophy, it has proved to be an effective route to recovery. Twelve-step groups are available worldwide, and some groups are tailored to specific eating disorders, for example Overeaters Anonymous.

Whereas organizations such as Weight Watchers focus on diet, calories and weighing, TSA does not address these matters but looks instead to explore the underlying emotional issues that are symptomized by the disordered eating behaviour.

This approach works on the principles of accepting our inevitable imperfections and personal responsibility for our choices, and acting flexibly rather than rigidly if we wish to change. It promotes humility to enable sufferers to reach out for help from others and encourages them to support and give hope to others to enable their recovery. Their mission statement is:

Working for H.E.A.L.T.H.
Honesty
Equality
Accountability
Love
Trust
Humility

13. Complementary therapies

What some call health, if purchased by perpetual anxiety
about diet, isn't much better than tedious disease.
George Dennison Prentice

Acupuncture

Acupuncture is an ancient form of traditional Chinese medicine in which fine needles are inserted into key points of the body, located along what are known as energy or meridian lines. It is not a stand-alone therapy for eating disorder treatment but is used as an adjunct to other psychological and or medical approaches.

The philosophy behind this treatment is that the manipulation of fine needles within various sites (which supposedly relate to specific organs in the body) will rebalance the body's energy flow. It is a holistic approach that can increase a client's sense of well-being on a physical and emotional level. The client's improved welfare is then believed to increase their receptiveness to formal treatments.

Acceptance and commitment therapy (ACT)

ACT is a derivative of cognitive behavioural therapy (CBT) that incorporates mindfulness. In ACT, the client is taught how to acquire a healthier attitude toward their body image and eating behaviours. By teaching mindfulness, in which clients become increasingly aware of their own thoughts and feelings, they become adept at early identification of destructive patterns and can choose not to react.

This level of insightfulness makes it easier for them to intercept and challenge the ingrained negative thought patterns that automatically lead to impulsive behaviours, such as bingeing and purging. By being aware of the triggers in their environment that activate negative body image beliefs and feelings, an individual can learn to apply a more positive and flexible attitude and can break destructive cycles of behaviour.

Hypnotherapy

Hypnotherapy is a very powerful tool for helping people to overcome eating disorders. By inducing a form of locked attention, a hypnotherapist can help a sufferer to focus on their problem in a heightened state of concentration. Hypnosis is an induced state of trance that artificially activates the brain's REM (rapid eye movement) state. While in this highly focused state, the hypnotherapist uses guided imagery to help induce a state of relaxation. The client is then better able to use the right hemisphere of the brain, which is creative, adept at problem-solving and capable of new learning.

Contrary to popular belief, hypnosis does not involve taking over someone else's mind. Hypnosis facilitates the individual's own ability to lock attention onto an idea and deal with it in a creative manner. In this way, new constructive forms of behaviour can be explored in a safe and non-threatening fashion. It is easy to visualize the potential of this form of treatment for someone who has been locked in negative eating habits like bingeing or laxative misuse.

Kinesiology

This is a form of energy work that seeks to rebalance the body's bio-energetic field to enable the body to heal. By using a combination of nutrition, energy reflexes, emotional techniques and massage, blockages in the energy flow are believed to be removed and the system is rebalanced. This holistic approach claims to be able to help discover the root cause of the client's problem, be it emotional, physical or chemical. This approach is used in conjunction with other treatments to address the eating disorder.

Massage

Clients with eating disorders often perceive their body as the enemy. Massage enables a client to experience their physical being in a pleasant and relaxing way, which helps to foster a more positive and healthy body image. The relaxation and releasing of tension in the body that accompanies massage also helps to reduce stress levels.

Remedial massage involves the masseur manipulating the client's body in a methodical, systematic manner, which serves to increase their dopamine and serotonin levels. Dopamine and serotonin play key roles in reward-motivated behaviour by contributing to feelings of happiness and well-being, which in turn help to alleviate depression.

Deep abdominal massage focuses on the tissue in this region, enabling tension to be released from both the reproductive and digestive systems. People suffering from bulimia in particular can find considerable relief in this form of massage as it can help to activate a sluggish digestive system.

Indian head massage is an ancient practice that is particularly effective in reducing stress and depression as well as decreasing insomnia in sufferers of eating disorders. Since it does not involve the removal of clothing or the need for a special massage table, it can be delivered in any environment and may be useful for sufferers who are uncomfortable about removing their clothes.

Meditation

Meditation can take many different formats, but all types help to promote self-acceptance and increase bodily awareness. Meditation provides the client with a means of self-soothing so that they can reduce their agitation by focusing on their breathing or repeating a mantra.

For clients with eating disorders, this adjunct to other therapies can help sufferers to reconnect with hunger signals and signals of satiety, with which they have lost touch. It is believed that by learning to transform their mental attitudes they will be able to release their own innate powers for self-healing.

By increasing self-awareness, meditation enables the

sufferer to arrest destructive eating patterns that have become habitual. Learning how to meditate is a hugely useful practice for people who have addictions and is therefore particularly helpful for those suffering from binge eating disorder.

Neurolinguistic programming (NLP)

Neurolinguistic programming is a treatment that seeks to change the language we use in our mind. By reprogramming our minds, we are able to impose new positive patterns of thought, which in turn enable us to change our behaviour and produce more constructive results.

This approach uses techniques such as hypnosis and positive affirmation to reprogramme the unconscious mind, disrupting deeply established bad habits and internalizing new beneficial habits.

A compulsive habit, such as self-induced vomiting after bingeing, is perpetuated as a consequence of the sufferer's self-perception. NLP reprogrammes the mind and attitude of the sufferer so that they can value themself differently and employ more constructive behaviours. Many people suffering from eating disorders find NLP to be very empowering, not only in helping them to conquer their eating disorder but also in their lives generally.

Reflexology

Reflexology is one of the most popular forms of bodywork – therapies and techniques in complementary medicine that involve touching or manipulating the body. Although there is no scientific proof to support this practice, there is a great wealth of anecdotal evidence that it promotes deep relaxation.

A reflexologist will apply pressure to various points on the ears, hands or feet, which allegedly represent other parts of the body. For example, the foot is divided up into various zones, each zone corresponding to the digestive system, heart or other organs. By applying a specific sequence of pressure to each zone, the aim is to rebalance the client's body.

Reiki

Reiki is another form of energy work, but it is different from other energy-based modalities in that it is applied with no specific intent, meaning the energy is non-directed. Reiki was used during the Gulf War as a way of increasing the sense of well-being of those in the military. It is a hands-on therapy that is quick and easy to apply.

By means of therapeutic touch, administered by the practitioner on the clothed body of the client, the body's energetic field is rebalanced; this promotes, calmness, clarity, relaxation and stress relief.

When used in conjunction with other forms of therapy, the soothing practice of reiki can help to empower sufferers of eating disorders to approach their recovery with greater mental, physical and emotional strength.

Yoga

Yoga refers to a range of physical, mental and spiritual disciplines practised in order to attain peace of mind or to reach a higher state of consciousness or enlightenment.

Yoga practice can be very useful for someone suffering from an eating disorder, since an individual with an eating disorder is so far removed from peace of mind and is certainly not in tune with their true self.

In addition, yoga provides an appropriate form of exercise, particularly suitable for those who compulsively exercise when their body does not possess sufficient calories to meet such strenuous demands. This is often the case for sufferers of anorexia, and gentler forms of yoga can provide a substitute to keep the body flexible and mobile.

Yoga promotes physical and mental self-awareness through physical movement, which helps the client to constructively reconnect with their body. Since sufferers of eating disorders have a jaundiced view of their body image, this can help ground them and achieve a greater degree of self-acceptance.

Furthermore, yoga can enable sufferers of eating disorders to become more consciously aware of pain signals from their body. I know of several over-exercisers who have continued to work out frenetically despite sprains, strains and blisters, seemingly unaware of their body's physical cues. Yoga helps reset this awareness and makes the sufferer less likely to exercise to a point that causes physical damage.

In most of these techniques, the underpinning science is largely irrelevant if the practice achieves a positive outcome. Taking care of oneself and feeling deserving of time and attention is in itself enormously therapeutic and increases self-esteem.

Sufferers of eating disorders often do not feel worthy of such attention, and the act of receiving and accepting care in this way is particularly beneficial in helping them to change their harsh attitudes towards themselves.

14. The Maudsley approach

*The greater the difficulty, the more
the glory in surmounting it.*
Epicurus

One of the forms of treatment I highly rate is known as the Maudsley approach. This is a family-based form of treatment that was originally devised to treat young patients under the age of eighteen who had suffered from anorexia for less than three years. This approach has also been shown to be very successful in helping sufferers of bulimia.

Dr Christopher Dare, along with colleagues at the London-based Maudsley Hospital, recognized that families could play a crucially supportive role in helping their children progress towards recovery. This is a most refreshing change in tack from the former, strongly held belief that the family is part of the problem. (It should be acknowledged that occasionally this *can* be the case, but is certainly not the norm.)

In this approach, the family are no longer demonized, in fact quite the opposite: they are seen as an asset and part of the solution. Empowered by specialist training in how to accompany a sufferer through the challenging stages of recovery, clinical trials have shown that family-based therapy is more successful than individual therapy. In addition, instead of the sufferer having to undergo expensive inpatient treatment, the Maudsley approach recommends they remain within the home.

I personally believe that the collaborative and supportive philosophy that underpins this approach makes it an effective foundation for the treatment of most problem eating. This is regardless of the age of the client/patient or the duration of the disorder, although it does most effectively lend itself to younger clients still living with their families. Having said this, partners and friends who assume the role of carer can also successfully engage in this approach with the sufferer's co-operation.

Intensive treatment in the home

In a nutshell, the Maudsley approach involves teaching the carer/family/friend a set of skills so that they can offer a form of outpatient treatment similar to the experience that nurses/therapists would offer within an inpatient setting. The family is taught how to externalize the illness: to see it as separate from the sufferer and as something that is beyond the sufferer's control.

In this programme, the sufferer of an eating disorder is treated in a similar way to a patient with a physical illness. We don't regard sufferers of mumps, measles or glandular fever as having control over their swellings, spots or temperature. By recognizing the eating disorder in this way, there is an immediate reduction in blame and frustration on the part of the family and shame and guilt on the part of the sufferer.

Benefits of this approach

It is easy to see the immediate benefits of this approach, in that it:

1. Is far cheaper than hospitalization.

2. Avoids the sufferer experiencing the potential trauma of being away from the home environment.

3. Obviates the need for re-integration into normal life after being discharged from an inpatient treatment, where patients frequently become institutionalized and the outside world can appear scary and threatening.

4. Provides the opportunity for underlying issues to be worked through with family support.

5. Prevents family members drifting apart by ensuring participation of all members, including siblings. Strong alliances between the sufferer and their siblings are actively encouraged by the treatment team.

6. Reduces the likelihood of other family members feeling neglected or jealous of the attention given to the sufferer since parents will not be frequently absent due to hospital visits.

7. Helps to de-pathologize the experience by maintaining normal activities for the sufferer, such as attending school or work, which would not be possible as an inpatient.

8. Provides support for all family members since the therapist will model non-judgemental and empathic

behaviour to create a non-blaming culture, which will help to establish acceptance and harmony within the family unit.

9. Teaches the family communication skills that will not only benefit them individually in their current situation, but will also have universal applications and benefits in other arenas.

10. Means lapses in recovery can be picked up very quickly due to the open communication and involvement of all family members. This enables the sufferer to gain immediate support to help them to get back on track at the earliest opportunity, rather than having to await appointments with medical personnel.

There are two important provisos for the use of this approach, as follows:

1. The sufferer must be medically stable

In all cases, this approach can only be used once the sufferer's critical physical condition has been stabilized. I use the term 'critical' to refer to the difference between life and death, that is, if the patient is so dangerously ill that they are in imminent danger of dying. At this point refeeding, rehydrating or other necessary medical interventions become the priority, since time is of the essence for preserving life. Once medical stabilization has been achieved, the Maudsley approach can be applied.

2. The family must be suitable for this approach

Not all families/households are suitable for this approach, since it demands a great deal of time, commitment, dedication and energy to support the sufferer. These resources may not always be available, even in the most well-intentioned families, particularly if both parents are full-time workers.

During the initial refeeding phase, caring can be like a full-time job, since every meal must be supervised. This may require a parent being available to bring their child home from school at lunchtime to ensure that the appropriate food intake is consumed and remains eaten.

Families where there is a high level of pre-existing dysfunction and discord would not be suitable for this approach, as seamless collaboration is essential. Even in the most well-adjusted families, the huge demands placed on parents, in both the planning and execution of the extra nursing role, can put a considerable strain on their own relationship.

In addition, there can still be misplaced guilt that your child being unwell is somehow your fault. This may be further aggravated by the ill-informed opinions of others who stigmatize parents of children that suffer from eating disorders. Thankfully, this ignorant attitude is on the wane, but it must always be borne in mind that in the same way the sufferer did not elect to contract an eating disorder and is not at fault, nor is the carer/parent to blame.

For this reason, it is essential that parents make arrangements for time out, putting another suitable adult temporarily in charge, so that they can attend to their own needs. As is the case for all carers – whether parents, friends, partners or siblings – neglect of their own needs, leisure pursuits and interests is not conducive to being able to offer patience and support as it can lead to exhaustion and demotivation.

Also, in families where parents or other siblings suffer from their own mental health issues, it would be a struggle to provide the environment required for this approach to be successful. Conversely, separated or divorced parents would not be precluded from this approach if prepared to work as a cohesive and united team.

However, if any family member were highly critical of the sufferer, it would totally undermine the ethos required for recovery and rehabilitation. It is inevitable that the sufferer will put up some resistance to eating; otherwise they could simply cure themself. Personalized criticism derails the process and totally hinders the treatment.

I will briefly describe how this form of treatment was applied to fifteen-year-old Lachlan and his parents, Clementine and Wayne. Lachlan had been suffering from anorexia for fourteen months before embarking upon this programme. The family undertook eighteen treatment sessions over a year and achieved a very successful outcome. (It is worth noting that studies have shown that this treatment is equally successful when conducted over six months, making it even more cost-effective.) Lachlan had to negotiate the following three stages in his journey to recovery.

Stage one: Weight restoration

Clementine and Wayne received training from Miguel, a trained specialist in the Maudsley approach, which empowered them to proceed with the treatment plan. It was explained that the creation of a non-hostile and affirming environment would be essential for Lachlan's recovery. This concept of harmony was taken on board by the entire family, all of whom worked collaboratively to promote this positive atmosphere.

Armed with the appropriate knowledge and skills, Lachlan's parents' first task was to focus solely on his weight restoration. They assumed total responsibility for ensuring that suitable meals were prepared and eaten by Lachlan. They were instructed that they must consistently enforce the agreed food rules without drama or threat, but that these rules were nonetheless totally non-negotiable. This responsibility by parents is essential, since a malnourished individual, particularly a child, is cognitively unstable and therefore incapable of making insightful decisions with regard to their own health needs.

Initially, having his power over what he ate removed proved to be very difficult for Lachlan. However, the intense encouragement and support he received from parents and siblings during this phase enabled Lachlan to achieve his weight goal. In fact, handing over the responsibility of what he had to eat eventually proved to be a relief to Lachlan, since he no longer had to deal with the anorexic voice in his head on his own.

Miguel attended some of the family meals and modelled the type of treatment Lachlan would have received had he been an inpatient. This involved empathizing with Lachlan's ambivalence about eating, while also endorsing firm expectations that weight restoration was not negotiable. Due to Miguel's coaching, Lachlan was never personally criticized for his challenging behaviour, the entire family accepted that this was all part of the disorder, and no fault was apportioned to him.

Having achieved his goal weight, Lachlan needed to demonstrate that he could maintain this weight on his own with little parental supervision. Stabilization is considered to have been achieved if the suffer has adopted the food guidelines and does not drop below 95 per cent of their target weight. Lachlan was successful in accomplishing this task and was therefore ready to move on to the next phase of his treatment.

Stage two: Return control over eating to the sufferer
Having surrendered full responsibility to his parents with regard to what and when he ate, the second stage consisted of gradually returning the control over eating to Lachlan. Reasserting autonomy can feel very alien for the sufferer at this stage, and they may struggle with taking back control and becoming more independent. Instead of receiving pre-plated meals, Lachlan was encouraged to serve himself under the watchful guidance of his parents.

One cannot underestimate the strong pull of the

disorder, and a great deal of family support is still required at this stage to prevent the sufferer from slipping back and losing the weight they have recently gained. Self-starvation is still a very real threat at this stage of recovery. Making sensible food selections and taking adequate portion sizes can feel very alien and threatening, particularly in restaurants where the range of choices can appear daunting.

As well as returning control of eating back to Lachlan, in this second phase the family was encouraged to address some of the tensions and issues that surrounded his problems with eating. During this stage, Lachlan was keen to attend a scout weekend with his friends, but his parents were concerned that having sole responsibility for his eating over two whole days might lead to a relapse. Aware that they should incentivize and motivate Lachlan to invest in activities rather than purely focus upon feeding, they settled upon a compromise.

They agreed that Clementine would deliver Lachlan and his younger brother to the camp straight after breakfast on both days and then Wayne would pick them both up in the evening. This compromise enabled Lachlan to take part in the weekend, which boosted his self-confidence. He successfully managed to take full responsibility for eating a sensible lunch on both days, while having the security of eating breakfast and dinner with his family.

With time, Lachlan became increasingly reliable in being able to maintain his target weight on his own. His parents allowed him to attend the following scout weekend full time and he openly admitted that although he could have skipped meals unnoticed he chose not to do so. This level of personal control signalled that the threat of self-starvation had abated enough for Lachlan to be ready to embark upon the final stage of the programme.

Stage three: Establish healthy identity
In this third stage, the task was for Lachlan to clarify his relationships within the family and come to terms with his changing identity as he progressed through adolescence. Adjustments of family boundaries were necessary to accommodate Lachlan's age-appropriate development towards adulthood and eventual independence.

With the support and guidance of Miguel, the family recognized the need to accommodate Lachlan's increasing maturity and need for autonomy, and the family dynamic adjusted accordingly. This phase is essential for long-term recovery since it is only by resolving the underlying emotional issues that relapse can be prevented. Sometimes individual therapy can prove to be useful at this point.

 As mentioned throughout this book, addressing the eating behaviour without dealing with the underlying cause is futile. It is like bandaging an untreated wound: it will only continue to fester and will never properly heal.

---

15. The carer's charter

I don't need a friend who changes when I change and
who nods when I nod; my shadow does that much better.
Plutarch

Listen and be consistent

Caring for someone with serious eating problems is one of the most exhausting things you can do. But it is essential that carers recognize that the sufferer is the only one who can decide they want to recover. It is futile to attempt to force them into submission, as this, at best, will be a temporary victory. Coercion, emotional blackmail and bullying will ultimately alienate the sufferer from your future support. The illness will inevitably reassert its grasp upon the sufferer if they have not signed up to the path of recovery of their own volition.

Hard as it may seem, avoid lecturing them on healthiness and what they should be doing for their own good. Instead, build trust and opportunities for them to talk to you freely. This will only happen if they know that you will not be laying down the law or passing judgement on them. Labelling and accusing just sets up power struggles. Recovery is very complex, and a sufferer cannot be forced into compliance if it is to be sustainable.

As a carer the biggest weapons that you have in your arsenal are consistency and your ability to listen. If you can listen with empathy and really enable the sufferer to feel truly heard then you have the basis for positive communication, which is the key to recovery.

 Communication is key. It is the sufferer's inability to communicate their needs in a healthy format that has led them to express themself so destructively in the first place.

Be patient
All you can do in the initial stage is to gently share your concerns and reassure them that you care. Be prepared for defensiveness and denial, and try to remain sanguine, since hostility will only create further resistance. You may have to raise the conversation several times before the person is ready to take your concerns on board. Do not take these rebuffs personally. Persevere but do not badger or hector.

Equally, it is important not to become submissive by walking on eggshells; gentle honesty is the only basis for good communication. Make clear which behaviours you find unacceptable, while stressing that it is the behaviour that has your disapproval, not the person. Recovery from an eating disorder is far more likely if the sufferer has a strong supportive social network, so exercising calmness and patience will yield dividends later.

Understand the change process

Use your influence wisely to encourage the sufferer to explore their situation so that they can identify for themself what works for them and what doesn't. The change process is gradual and can only successfully progress when the sufferer is ready for each stage.

I once read that recovering from an eating disorder was similar to a play with the following acts:

Act one: Initially the eating disorder seems to work for the sufferer and appears to assuage their problems. At the end of the act, the realization dawns upon the sufferer that living with the eating disorder is no longer a viable option, and they recognize how dysfunctional their life has become.

Act two: The sufferer begins to explore ways of possible recovery in a half-hearted manner, while still holding onto the eating disorder. They try out various experiments and strategies but don't do them seriously. This act ends when they appreciate that recovery will only be achieved when they are fully committed and determined to go down that route. They recognize that they cannot have both worlds and decide they want to forsake the eating disorder.

Act three: The sufferer pursues a focused and determined approach to recovery, and no matter how many times they falter, they pick themself up and persist towards their goal. They eventually acquire the necessary skills, support and knowledge to defeat the eating disorder. The act, and the play, ends when long-term recovery is established. At this point, the sufferer is no longer simply a player, but a director in the next act of their life.

Be ready

Try to educate yourself as much as possible so that when the sufferer is no longer in denial you will be ready to share information with them. As well as acquiring knowledge about problematic eating, there is nothing to stop you from expressing your concerns to a counsellor or GP, or visiting a self-help group.

By arming yourself with the necessary knowledge and skills to support the sufferer, you can capitalize on their readiness to embrace change in that moment. However, it is important that you travel at the pace set by the sufferer, as they may have just moved from the pre-contemplation stage to that of contemplation. Being too eager to sally forth into recovery planning will only scare the horses.

Remain calm and assertive

People with eating disorders can be incredibly challenging and can appear to be very selfish since they lose their ability to empathize. It can be very trying when someone has stolen money or eaten other people's food. The bathroom may be left in a dreadful state, food may be hidden under the sofa and empty food packaging may be littered all over the house.

It is important that you explain the needs of other members of the household and consistently apply family rules in an assertive, unaggressive manner. Other family members need access to the bathroom to get ready for school or work, and it will only build resentment if the sufferer is dictating how everyone else must fit in with their needs.

There is often a temptation to capitulate rather than risk a scene, since the eating disorder can sometimes turn the sufferer into a bully. It is not in anyone's best interest that the household is held to ransom. This will only make the eating disorder more powerful. If a heated exchange takes place, rather than allowing it to escalate, insist on taking 'time out' for everyone to calm down. Later, when people are less emotional and het up, have a discussion about the disagreement and see if you can forge a joint understanding of expectations.

Help to build self-esteem

Remind the sufferer that recovery involves rebuilding their self-esteem. Encourage them to learn to really listen to their feelings and their body. For example, the statement 'I feel fat' can be deconstructed with your help and further explored by asking: 'What does that mean to you?' The reply might be, 'I feel unacceptable' or 'unlovable' or 'disgusted by myself'.

Help them to work towards self-acceptance and to learn to trust themself. It is important that they learn not to be frightened of their powerful emotions and that they use people they trust to comfort them, rather than food (or lack of it). Encourage them to recognize their strengths rather than exclusively focusing on their weaknesses. Remind them of their accomplishments, abilities and talents, as well as helping them to challenge negative self-talk. Constant affirmation of any positive behaviour, no matter how small, is a very effective tool. Remember that 'success breeds success'.

Constructive ways to vent emotions

Help the sufferer to explore more positive ways of dealing with feelings of upset or disappointment, rather than taking it out on their body by self-harming, starvation, bingeing and purging. Ideas that they may come up with could be listening to favourite music, going for a walk with the dog, calling a good friend, going to the cinema, playing a favourite game, helping someone else, going for a massage, having a manicure, enjoying a deep bubble bath or occupying themself with a hobby.

The more fulfilling and enjoyable their life becomes, the less time they will spend ruminating and being self-critical. Help them to explore why they feel they must be 'perfect' and must adhere to strict eating rules, and why they think their weight should dictate their sense of value and worthiness. If you do this in a diplomatic way without expectation or judgement you will not create resistance.

Refuse to collude with the eating disorder

Always avoid going head-to-head with the eating disorder. So in response to questions such as 'Do I look fat?' you simply reply along the lines of: 'That's not a healthy topic of conversation, and I'm far more interested in hearing about how your day went.'

Also, do not be a vigilante by monitoring and over-questioning the sufferer's food intake. Being constantly watched will just lead to greater levels of subterfuge and deception, risking damage to the relationship. If the person is not ready to give up excessive exercising, bingeing and purging, then all the surveillance in the world will not stop them. Of course, it's an entirely different matter if they have requested your help, such as sitting with them while they eat to encourage them to finish their meal.

Assist in identifying triggers

Help the sufferer to identify the triggers that precipitate destructive behaviours so that they can learn to avoid them or cope with them more constructively. Triggers might be things like looking at fashion magazines, going on a beach holiday, weighing themselves, being invited to a ball, exams and the stress of revision, visiting websites that encourage eating disorders, attending interviews, mixing with 'toxic' friends – the possibilities are endless. Encouraging the sufferer to keep a journal can be very useful, as it can help to identify triggers and outline the accompanying feelings.

Encourage autonomy

When they are ready to seek help, ask how they would like you to support them. They may wish you to accompany them on a visit to their GP or a self-help group or ask you to investigate various clinics, therapies or therapists. It is important that you work with them rather than seizing control. The only way to build self-esteem is to encourage an individual's autonomy and self-trust.

Tempting as it may seem to grab the reins once you have received the green light from the sufferer, it is important to resist this urge. Long-term recovery is only possible with the sufferer at the helm, so encourage this from the start. By working collaboratively and showing your confidence in their ability to take the necessary steps towards recovery, you will foster self-reliance and self-confidence.

Support during lapses

Having found the right help, your continued support will be invaluable in helping the sufferer stick to their prescribed treatment plan. At times of low mood it will be difficult for them to continue with what they have agreed to do and they will inevitably lapse. By being able to help them to accept that lapses are part of the road to recovery, you will be instrumental in preventing them from quitting the treatment plan.

It is often after significant successes that the illness reasserts itself, and in such instances the sufferer feels their failure acutely. Remind them how far they have come already and that nobody is perfect, and offer consistent support and encouragement to help them continue. Recording setbacks and constantly reviewing progress is a very useful aid since this documentation will eventually show that the lapses are becoming shorter and less frequent.

Look after yourself

Caring for someone with an eating disorder is phenomenally challenging and it is very easy to find that your entire life revolves around their progress towards recovery or lack of it. It is vital that you do not allow this focus to consume you and other members of the family. It is essential that you continue to have a social life and enjoy the support of your friends.

When trying to give so much energy, attention and compassion to the person for whom you are caring, you need to make sure that your own batteries are fully charged if you are to go the distance. Share responsibilities with family members and friends so that everyone gets some respite and a chance to indulge in their hobbies and interests.

This will not only increase your capacity to cope but will also reduce the guilt that the sufferer may feel at witnessing their family losing touch with friends and activities. By demonstrating self-care you will also be leading by example. Providing a positive role model will serve to encourage the sufferer to see themself more holistically rather than purely in relation to their food intake.

Hope and belief

The most important ingredient of all for a successful recovery is *hope* and *belief* that recovery is possible. Sadly, in cases where the nurse, medical practitioner or carer lacks this faith, recovery is often seriously undermined. Many people see eating disorders as self-inflicted and the sufferers as untrustworthy and manipulative, which destroys the quality of the helping relationship.

If you know that you cannot offer these vital ingredients then do not attempt to carry out the role of carer since you will inevitably do more harm than good.

On the other hand, you do not have to be perfect; if you approach the sufferer with respect, care and love, you are giving them the best chance of recovery that you can.

Final thought

Suffering from problem eating can cause a great deal of emotional distress as well as physical damage. I hope that by reading this little book you feel empowered to tackle your difficulties around food by addressing the underlying issues, or that you are ready to take the first step towards seeking help, either for yourself or for someone you are concerned about. Remember that you are far from alone, so don't suffer in silence and allow the problem to increasingly detract from your quality of life. Try to have the courage to take that initial step by picking up the phone and making an appointment to see your doctor. Or perhaps the right first step for you is to confide in a member of your family or a friend in whom you can trust. Alternatively, you might prefer to contact a helpline and speak to someone who is trained to understand your concerns around eating.

Just think about what you could do with all the extra time and energy you would have if you were not constantly worrying about your food intake. Remember to be your own best friend by recognizing that you are so much more than your problem eating. I wish you all the courage that you need to take the necessary action to challenge your problem eating and defeat it.

Be in no doubt, problem eating can be overcome.

Useful contacts

UK

Men Get Eating Disorders Too
Tel: 08456 341 414
www.mengetedstoo.co.uk

Support and Education for Eating Disorders
Tel: 08443 915 539
www.facebook.com/groups/seedpreston

Support and Empathy for People with Eating Disorders
Tel: 01482 718 130
www.seedeatingdisorders.org.uk

Maudsley Parents
www.maudsleyparents.org

Beat
Tel: 08456 341 414
www.b-eat.co.uk

National Centre for Eating Disorders
Tel: 08458 382 040
www.eating-disorders.org.uk

Norfolk Eating Disorders Association
Tel: 01603 767 062
www.eatingmatters.org.uk

Somerset and Wessex Eating Disorders Association
Tel: 01749 671 318
www.swedauk.org

Young Minds
Tel: 08088 025 544
www.youngminds.org.uk

National Institute for Health Care Excellence
www.nice.org.uk

British Association for Behavioural and Cognitive Psychotherapies
Tel: 01617 054 304
www.babcp.com

British Association for Counselling and Psychotherapy
Tel: 01455 883 316
Email: bacp@bacp.co.uk
www.bacp.co.uk

British Psychological Society
Tel: 01162 549 568
Email: enquiry@bps.org.uk
www.bps.org.uk

Patricia Furness-Smith
Tel: 01494 766 246
www.maturus.co.uk

Eating Disorders Support
Tel: 01494 793 223
Email: support@eatingdisorderssupport.co.uk
www.eatingdisorderssupport.co.uk

National Counselling Society
Tel: 08708 503 389
www.nationalcounsellingsociety.org

The Mental Health Foundation
Tel: 02078 031 100
Email: mhf@mhf.org.uk
www.mentalhealth.org.uk

I-Eat
Tel: 07590 378 822
www.i-eat.org.uk

Scottish Eating Disorders Interest Group
www.sedig.co.uk

Managed Clinical Network for Eating Disorders
Tel: 01224 557 858
www.nhsgrampian.org

See Me Scotland
Tel: 01315 166 819
www.seemescotland.org.uk

Counselling & Psychotherapy in Scotland
Tel: 01786 475 140
www.cosca.org.uk

Ireland
Irish Health
www.irishhealth.com

Body Whys: The Eating Disorder Association of Ireland
Tel: 1890 200 444
www.bodywhys.ie

Psychological Society of Ireland
Tel: 01 472 0105
www.psihq.ie

Canada
British Columbia Eating Disorders Association
Tel: 250 383 2755 or 250 383 5518
www.webhome.idirect.com/~bceda/index.html

New Zealand
Eating Disorders Association
Tel: 09 5222 679
Email: anorexia@xtra.co.nz
www.ed.org.nz

New Zealand Psychological Society
Tel: 04 473 4884
www.psychology.org.nz

Australia
National Eating Disorders Collaboration
Tel: 1800 33 4673
www.nedc.com.au

Eating Disorders Association (Queensland)
Tel: (07) 3891 3660 or 3394 3661
www.eda.org.au

Australian Association for Cognitive and Behaviour Therapy
www.aacbt.org

Australian Psychological Society
Tel: (03) 8662 3300 or 1800 333 497
www.psychology.org.au

USA
Mental Fitness, Inc.
www.normal-life.org

Binge Eating Disorder Association
Tel: 855 855 2332
www.bedaonline.com

The National Eating Disorders Association
Tel: 1800 931 2237
www.nationaleatingdisorders.org

Eating Disorders Coalition
Tel: 202 543 9570
www.eatingdisorderscoalition.org

National Association of Anorexia Nervosa and Associated Disorders
Tel: 630 577 1330
www.anad.org

American Psychological Association
Tel: (202) 336 6024 or (800) 374 2721
www.apa.org

South Africa
Eating Disorders South Africa
Tel: 012 993 1060
www.eatingdisorderssa.com

Psychological Society of South Africa
Tel: 011 486 3322
www.psyssa.com

South African National Association of Practicing Psychologists
Tel: 011 485 2596
www.sanapp.co.za

Acknowledgements

I am hugely indebted to my dearest friends and family for all their love and practical support, which has kept me going while writing this book. I have needed you and want you to know how greatly I have valued your kindness and will always cherish our friendships.

I extend my gratitude to all of my clients who have shared their darkest hours with me while they have struggled with their problem eating. They have taught me the power of the human spirit in overcoming what can feel like insurmountable mountains to climb. Despite the many setbacks on their journeys to recovery, they have recognized that to falter is not to fail. They have clung tenaciously to hope, persevered and triumphed and scaled those mountains and overcome their illnesses. I salute their courage and determination.

I thank all at Icon Books for giving me the opportunity to increase public awareness about problem eating. I am passionate that people should comprehend this greatly misunderstood range of mental health disorders and this book has given me a voice towards that end. In particular, I am grateful to my editors Kate Hewson and Kiera Jamison and assistant editor Nira Begum for their guidance, as well as to Mark Ecob for designing the book's jacket, Robert Sharman for his careful proof reading and Christopher Summerville for compiling the index.

My special thanks go to Dr Charlotte Wing, friend and colleague, who has shared with me her considerable insights into eating disorders. My appreciation also goes to Gwen Milligan for her eternal patience in facilitating my research.

My deepest and most heartfelt thanks go to my darling husband, Charles, and my inspirational son, Alex, both of whom have taught me forbearance and courage. Finally, I would like to thank my inimitable muse, Buffy, a veritable force of nature whose joyous enthusiasm, generosity of spirit and unparalleled sweetness will echo eternally throughout the rest of my life and those of many others.

Index